GRC in BFS Industry

(A beginner's guide on **G**overnance, **R**isk Management and **C**ompliance by **B**anking & **F**inance Industry)

*

Dr. Ramamurthy N.
M.Sc., B.G.L., CAIIB, CCP, DSADP, CISA, PMP, CGBL, Ph.D.

*

*

Title: **GRC in BFS Industry**
(A beginner's guide on **G**overnance, **R**isk Management
and **C**ompliance by Banking & Finance Industry)

First Edition: May 2020

Author: **Dr. Ramamurthy N,**
http://ramamurthy.jaagruti.co.in/

Number of pages: 174

ISBN (13): 978-93-82237-60-0

*****

Table of Contents

*****

Dedication

This book is being dedicated to the entire Banking & Financial Service Industry of the globe which has brought the author to this level.

Dr. Ramamurthy N

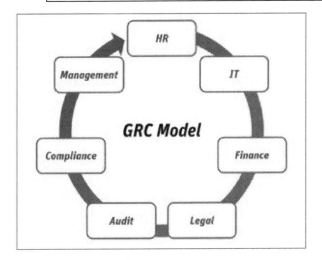

*****

N Raja B.com., FCA, DISA, Partner,
N Raja & Associates, Flat No 8 1st Floor V K Manor,
New No 8 Old No 28, Gopalakrishna Road, T Nagar,
Chennai – 600 017, India,
Mobile: +91 94440 84850, email: nrajaca@hotmail.com

Foreword

GRC — Governance, Risk and Compliance — is an umbrella term for the processes and practices that organizations implement to meet business objectives through;

- Identifying potential Risks
- Monitoring and mitigating risks
- Tracking regulatory change and verifying compliance
- Aligning policies and processes to achieve organizational goals

GRC-This jargon is probably a decade+ old. However, GRC management has come a long way from binders with full of documentation, unwieldy spreadsheets, and other manual processes. Rather than just a catchall term for unconnected management activities, truly integrated GRC — sometimes referred to as integrated risk management — takes a holistic, enterprise-wide approach to understanding risks and opportunities to better support organizational strategy.

For GRC management to be successful in today's business landscape, it must be technology-enabled to adapt to changing needs and equip teams to manage, monitor, and act on risk in real time.In short, effective GRC should be strategic, integrated, and digitized.

- GRC is strategic when it in equips leadership to make informed, risk-based decisions that align with business objectives.
- GRC technology is only helpful inasmuch as it is used in conjunction with good processes. Once organizations have strong policies and procedures in place, investing in a GRC solution can assist in making significant improvements in organizational performance, decision-making, risk awareness, and digital transformation.

Dr.Ramamurthy, a friend of mine a retired Banker, Certified Information System Auditor (CISA) has vast experience in Banking risk management, compliance and has been advising many clients on risk management. He has been offering IT solutions for Risk Management with his practical experience. It is a nice idea that he has come out with this book for beginners. Many fundamental concepts are dealt with, in simple terms and in lucid style for easier understanding and that is the specialty of this book.It has been mentioned as "if you do not update yourself, you will be outdated". This is very much true in the fast phase of technological development.We need to update on every topic, we go through. Especially risk management and laws to be complied with, are highly volatile. Everyone needs to update themselves on a constant and continuous basis.

There cannot be a generic GRC solution across industry. Hence this book can be used as a fundamental guide.

Depending on the industry or organization, the reader is into, he has to improve it further. I am sure this book will be very useful for the readers and especially the beginners.

I am amazed that **Dr. Ramamurthy** has penned 43 books so far and more are in the pipeline. The topics of his books are varied. This shows his versatility. I wish him a healthy long life and success in his endeavors. Also request him to share his knowledge and 43+ years of experience by coming out with more books. Best wishes to all the readers.

Chennai
May 2020   N. Raja

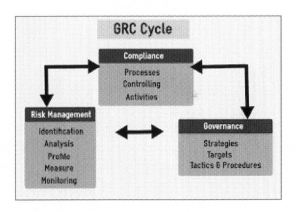

* * * * *

Introduction

GRC (**G**overnance, **R**isk Management and **C**ompliance) is the umbrella term covering any organization's approach across these three areas. Being closely related concerns, Governance, Risk Management and Compliance activities are increasingly being integrated and aligned to some extent in order to avoid conflicts, wasteful overlaps and gaps. While interpreted differently in various organizations, GRC typically encompasses activities such as Corporate Governance, Enterprise Risk Management (ERM) and Corporate Compliance with applicable laws, regulations, standards, etc.

> *GRC typically encompasses activities such as Corporate Governance, Enterprise Risk Management (ERM) and Corporate Compliance with applicable laws, regulations, standards, etc.*

Governance describes the overall management approach through which senior executives direct and control the entire organization, using a combination of management information and hierarchical management control structures. Governance activities ensure that critical management information reaching the executive team is adequately complete, accurate and timely to enable appropriate management decisions and provide the control mechanisms to ensure that strategies, directions and instructions from management are carried out systematically and effectively. Normal management runs an organization, but the leaders manage the organization and Visionary leaders govern the organization – Proactive governance is the leadership quality and that is the need of the hour.

Risk Management is the set of processes through which management identifies, measures, analyzes and wherever necessary, responds appropriately to risks that might adversely affect realization of the organization's business objectives. The response to risks typically depends on their perceived gravity and involves controlling, avoiding, accepting or transferring them to a third party. Whereas banks routinely manage a wide range of risks (e.g. Credit Risk, Market Risk, Operational Risk, Forex Risk, Technology Risk, Information Security Risk and what not), external legal and regulatory compliance risks are arguably the key issues in GRC.

Compliance means conforming with stated requirements mostly by the legal system. At an organizational level, it is achieved through management processes which identify the applicable requirements (defined by laws, regulations, contracts, strategies, policies and so on), assess the state of compliance, assess the risks and potential costs of non-compliance against the projected expenses to achieve compliance and hence prioritize, fund and initiate any corrective actions deemed necessary.

GRC is an increasingly recognized term that reflect a new way in which organizations are adopting an integrated approach to these aspects of the business.

Integrated GRC

Integrated GRC can refer to either;

1. eGRC (enterprise wide GRC) that allows the impact of multiple primary regulations to be tracked and correlated to a single system and/ or

2. GRC systems based on Information Technology that can take information feeds from multiple sources that detect or sense deviations, defects or other patterns from security or business applications. This can include active sensor technologies such as those to protect, monitor and manage information networks and systems. By combining GRC technologies such as web-based information security management systems with network security related sensor technologies via the interface protocol, that defenses against cyber-attacks are enhanced.

It is also possible to combine both these levels through a single platform.

eGRC has a much higher-level focus, correlating more with the ability to detect and prevent regulatory compliance issues that can lead to reputational damage and punitive financial penalties.

The micro form uses "active sensor platforms", there are currently multiple standards. There are also moves to try to standardize the approach — although a challenge is that this market is still maturing and yet to evolve. One open standard is termed as "governance, risk and compliance inter-operability protocol".

GRC research

The first scholarly research on GRC was published in 2007 and defined as "the integrated collection of capabilities that enable an organization to reliably achieve objectives, address uncertainty and act with integrity."

A survey carried out in 2019 found that there is hardly any scientific research on GRC as of today. The GRC administrators went on to derive the first scientifically grounded GRC short-definition from an extensive literature review. Subsequently the definition was validated in a survey among GRC professionals and came with the conclusion that "GRC is an integrated, holistic approach to organization-wide governance, risk and compliance ensuring that an organization acts ethically correct and in accordance with its risk appetite, internal policies and external regulations through the alignment of strategy, processes, technology and people, thereby improving efficiency and effectiveness". Then this definition was translated into a frame of reference for GRC research. Governance, Risk Management and Compliance are the core disciplines of GRC. Each of the disciplines consists of the four basic components viz.: strategy, processes, technology and people. The bank's risk appetite, its internal policies and external regulations constitute the rules of GRC. The disciplines, their components and rules are to be merged in an integrated, holistic and organization-wide (the three main characteristics of GRC) manner – aligned with the operations that are managed and supported through GRC.

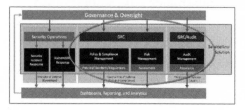

In applying this approach, banks long to achieve the objectives of GRC; ethically right behaviour and improved efficiency and effectiveness of all the elements involved.

GRC is a sprouting concept. Understanding it in its entirety, providing solutions, etc., are not so easy. Still an analysis and understanding by segmentation would enable the banks to take proactive steps and govern the risks and the compliance areas. This book is trying a step towards this. Though the first aim of this book is BFS industry per se, in general the discussions are applicable to any industry as a whole.

This book is intended to be a beginner's (for dummies) guide. Hence most of the concepts, ideas, etc., discussed in this book related almost all the industries. However, based on the personal experience of the author, the specifics discussed in detail relate to BFS Industry and in particular Banking industry. The concepts discussed in this book, if need to be completely explained, need separate book for each of the areas. They are just touched upon to kindle the thought process of the readers. Further enlightenment can be had by reading separate books. To cater to fast moving world the concepts are explained as bullets and through diagrams as well rather than paragraphs. One more caution in this regard – these areas are very volatile and need to be kept updated. If we do not update ourselves, we will be outdated.

Auditors are more knowledgeable on GRC. Hence it is very apt that an auditor gives a foreword to this book. The author is thankful to Mr. Raja, auditor for the nice introduction and foreword with some pleasantries about the book and the author.

Thanks a lot for all those who supported from the behind in bringing out this book. Readers are request to feel free to send the comments/ Remarks.

Chennai
May 2020   *Dr. Ramamurthy N*

*****

Managing for Results

The single goal of every business, be it in any industry, is 'results' − more specifically "economic results" and still more specifically "economically positive results", which means profit. To obtain the profit the business has to be 'managed' or in modern terms 'governed'.

> *The single goal of every business, be it in any industry, is 'results' − "economically positive results", which means profit.*

One of the major universal issues with today's governance is that management do not give adequate time neither sufficient thought to the future. Today's tasks take all the executives' time and yet it is seldom done well. It is felt that they are all in rat's race and managed by the mails in the 'in' box (earlier days in tray). The crash programs attempting to 'solve' the 'urgent' problems do not achieve right and lasting results. When these 'urgent' problems seem to be resolved they are all happy and try to attack the next 'urgent' problem. Mostly these are 'crisis' management.

If the management wants to tackle the future, the challenges of today have to be disposed off in lesser time and with greater impact, permanence and forethought.

The economic tasks can be approached in a three-dimensional way;

1. The present business must be made effective.
2. The potential has to be identified and realized.

3. The business has to be made differently for the different future.

Each of the above has variety of questions and have to be approached distinctively. However, they are inseparable. All the three have to be attacked simultaneously and in an integrated way – i.e. today, it can never be tomorrow.

The resources and hence the results cannot be searched inside the business. They exist outside. There are no profit centers within the business – all are cost centers. Any business activity be it engineering, selling, manufacturing or accounting, etc., they all incur costs. Their contribution to profit is the key to be managed. Results do not depend on anything or anybody within nor within the control of anyone. They depend on something/ somebody outside – the customer, what is called the "market economy".

Results can be expected by exploiting the opportunities and not by problem resolutions or crisis management. Most of management's time is spent only on resolving the problems. Resolution of a problem to restore normalcy. The very SWOT analysis is meant for converting the Weaknesses to Strength and the Threats to Opportunities. If some productive time is spent on the future strategies and exploitation of opportunities – the results will automatically be achieved. Resources should be prudently allocated focusing the opportunities. It is not that the

> *The resources and hence the results cannot be searched inside the business. They exist outside. There are no profit centers within the business – all are cost centers.*

problems can be shrug off, but minimum resources should be utilized for resolving problems and more resources for concentrating opportunities. Opportunities do not occur themselves – they have to be created and knocks only once. It is for the management to grab it at the first knocking itself. There helps the creative thinking, diagonal thinking and so on.

Economic results are earned only by prudent governance. It cannot be got just like that. It cannot be taken for granted. It is not by mere competence. Profits are the rewards for making a unique or at least a distinct, meaningful contribution. What is meaningful? Who can decide it? Only the customer can decide. The definition of meaningful may vary from industry to industry, organization to organization, customer to customer. The business has to provide some value, the market can accept and is willing to pay a price for the same. Monopoly type of business is an exception in this case. This in no way means that the business establishment has to be a giant in that industry – no need. Being big is not synonymous with governance. But an organization, which wants to get economic results has to have governance in something of real value to a customer or market. Consequently, this ends up with having good leadership. It may seem to have a leader, a large share of the market, full weight of momentum, history and tradition. But the question is "is it capable of survival in the long run", let alone of getting profits.

The institution/ organization has to understand that "any leadership position is transitory and likely to be short lived". No business can ever secure a permanent leader.

For a leader the energy always tends towards diffusion. Business tends to drift from governance to mediocrity. It is the executive's role to reverse the drift and focus the business on opportunity and away from problems.

> "any leadership position is transitory and likely to be short lived". No business can ever secure a permanent leader.

What exists is getting old. The management team do not try to resolve today's problems. They spend most of their time in trying to resolve yesterday's problems. This, by and large, is inevitable. However, less time and effort need be spent on this and more focus on tomorrow. Forward looking thoughts, decisions and actions are the need of the hour. The forward-looking strategy cannot be a static one – it has to be a dynamic one depending on the needs of the market. Events do not happen as expected. As generals do prepare for the war, the businessmen always tend to react in terms of the last boom or depression and hence it is yesterdays. Any decision or action starts to get old the moment it has been made. The job is to change the business, its behavior, its attitude, its expectations, possibly the products and the markets – channels to fit the new realties.

Business enterprise is not a phenomenon of nature but one of society – what exists is misallocated. Events are not distributed according to "normal distribution". Always there exists an 80-20 rule. 20% of the customers contributing to 80% of the profit and 80% of the customers contributing to 20% of the profit. Similarly, 20% of the events account for 80% of the results and 80% of the events account for 20% of the results. This practically holds for all problems.

Another perspective to the above rule is – resources and efforts are generally allocated themselves to 80% of the events that practically produce no results. They are automatically allocated to events that without any results. Many organizations' salesmen are misallocated. Their efforts are wasted on products that are hard to sell,

> *20% of the customers contributing to 80% of the profit and 80% of the customers contributing to 20% of the profit. Similarly, 20% of the events account for 80% of the results and 80% of the events account for 20% of the results.*

because they are yesterday's products. The organizations cannot sell what they have – they have to sell what the market/ customers need. Tomorrow's important products rarely need any sales effort and they automatically sensationally succeed.

Chapter Summary;

The single goal of every business, be it in any industry, is 'results' – "economically positive results", which means profit.

The resources and hence the results cannot be searched inside the business. They exist outside. There are no profit centers within the business – all are cost centers.

"Any leadership position is transitory and likely to be short lived". No business can ever secure a permanent leader.

20% of the customers contributing to 80% of the profit and 80% of the customers contributing to 20% of the profit. Similarly, 20% of the events account for 80% of the results and 80% of the events account for 20% of the results.

	Managing by Means	Managing by Results
Process	• Focus is on the means by which goals are achieved. • Means are seen as "ends-in-the-making."	• Focus is on the performance of separate parts of the organization. • Ends are seen as top priority in and of themselves.
View of the Organization	• The company is a network of patterns and relationships connecting people with each other, and with customers, the community and the ecosystem.	• The company is a machine that can be made to perform better overall through optimization of the performance of its separate parts.
Parts/Wholes	• Focus is on how the whole system performs.	• Focus is on how each separate part performs.
Assumptions About Profit	• Profit is necessary for the company's survival but is not the company's reason for existing.	• Profit is the overall goal and purpose of the organization. • The company must maximize profit above all else.
Control	• Emphasis on local decision-making and responsibility; parts of the system have their own wisdom.	• Emphasis on centralized decision-making and goal-setting; parts of the system will respond only to external force.

*****

Landscape of an Organization

Before actually plunging into governance, it would be a good idea to ponder and have a grip of the organization – its landscape, organizational structure – phycological behavior of the people working in the organization, etc.

Organizational **landscapes** *are composed of a collection of functions which are organized in the organization. They include small-scale function/ department onwards major technological dependency.*

What is an Organizational Landscape? Organizational **landscapes** are composed of a collection of functions which are organized in the organization. They include small-scale function/ department onwards major technological dependency. Organizational landscape colloquially called as "organization structure" affects the organizational actions and provides the foundation on which standard operating procedures and routines rest. It determines which individuals get to participate in which decision-making processes and thus to what extent their views shape the organization's actions. Organizational structure can also be considered as the viewing glass or perspective through which individuals see their organization and its environment. A typical organization structure would be like – irrespective of industry;

It was mentioned that colloquially called as organization structure and organizational landscape are synonymous. However, at a high level they are different. Organization structure will be role/ position based and organizational landscape would be section/ department based. There is not department or section without the people working in it – that is the various positions/ roles in those section/ department. In that angle, organization structure and organizational landscape can be treated as same. A typical organizational landscape would be;

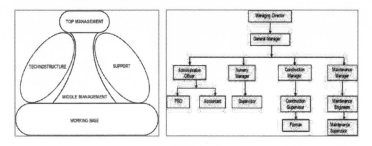

Figure 1 – Typical Organization Structures

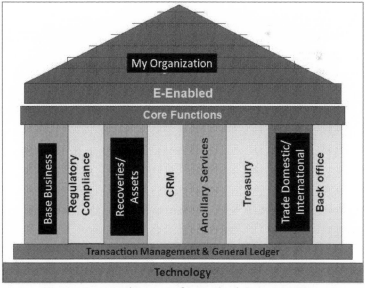

Figure 2 – Landscape of a typical Organization

How Really Things Work in an organization - To be effective, we need to clearly understand the way the organization actually works - as opposed to the way we wish it might work or think it should work). Especially important is knowing what the organizational values (stated or unstated) and how decisions are made.

What Is Most Valued? - People in organizations pay attention to what the organization most values. At its most basic, this is about understanding the essential elements of the organization's culture. With the answers to the below questions one may conclude what is most valued;

- Is this a mission-centric or customer-centric organization?
- Is it a support organization that is most concerned with keeping the hierarchy around it happy and satisfied?
- What kinds of ideas do people pay attention to and what is usually dismissed
- Has the organization endured a recent trauma that is leading everyone to play it safe, or alternatively, has a leader encouraging bold ideas?

From the conclusion of what is most valued, an opinion of positioning the ideas can be made. Are customers most valued? If so, can ideas and customers be linked in some way? Are ideas about administrative issues, such as parking, not valued? For example, happier employees will go the extra mile to help customers. The more the link can be established with what the organization values, the more likely it is that the idea would be considered.

It is Not Easy Being Always Green – This concept is better and clearly understood with the following instance;

In one of the organizations the CEO pointed out that the company was using 100 percent virgin plastics for all its packaging, which conflicted with the company's recently defined green initiatives.

On a Monday the CEO held discussions about moving to recycled plastic (which uses 70 percent less energy in the manufacture). There was great resistance from within along the lines of "too hard" and "can't do it now, costs too much". The CEO pressed his point that it was a little incongruous to have newly defined vision, mission and values only to reject movement towards a more sustainable future at the very first hurdle. A long conversation with the plastic bottle and tub manufacturer ensued and issues of supply and quality were raised.

By Friday of that week, the organization had working samples and a provisional agreement for 100 percent recycled plastic pellets in the three plastics we needed and the change was made at no extra cost. The toolmaker was also consulted to thin the walls of the packaging without affecting structural performance, thus saving more plastic. One week to dramatically change the direction and performance of the company. Subsequently, the organization won Gold at the Australian Packaging Awards in the Export Category for our commitment to the environment and were recognized by Sustainability Victoria.

How Are Decisions Made? – Let us look at how decisions are made overall. Is the organization surprisingly democratic in its processes and does it value consensus? Or is there a strong executive who has the authority to make command decisions? Does it have many independent power centers or is there more of a traditional hierarchy? Who influences whom?

Knowing this helps determine the people with whom the relationships need to be built. As the relationships are built, what is important to those people and their organizations can be decided. By doing so, the ideas to what is important to those decision makers can be connected. For instance, if the steering committee that makes decisions about technology is intent on reducing complexity, shows how the idea reduces complexity. If HR decision makers are looking to attract a younger demographic, show how the idea will appeal to millennials.

Why Do People Say No? - Mastering the organizational landscape also means finding out why people say no. Here are some tools that can be used to explore where the resistance is coming from;

- **The Five Whys** - The "five whys" is a useful approach for getting at cause-effect relationships behind problems or resistance to new ideas. A five-why analysis might proceed as –

> *One has to understand the phycology of the people before clearly define how to govern*

- Why does X oppose the idea? Is it disruptive?
- Why does X think it is disruptive? It would mess with the sales process.

- Why does X think it would mess with the sales process? Because it would make it harder to keep metrics.
- Why does X think it would be harder to keep metrics? Because salespeople will be spending all their time on the new approach.
- Why would salespeople have to spend all their time? Because salespeople aren't good enough writers to prepare the consumer sentiment analysis what is wanted.

By exploring at least five "whys" questions in the analysis, one can go deep enough to uncover the real implementation problems for the idea[1].

As a first step to understand the phycology of the people answers to five whys has to be understood.

What is The Perspective? - Another approach is perspective taking: the ability to see things from others' perspectives. Too many of the people run into a dead end because the ideas are pushed forward based on how they see the situation without stopping to consider the decision makers' viewpoints. Understanding what it is like to be them can give clues to how to position the idea — or how likely the idea is to be considered.

Organizations are made up of people. All change affects people. One may have a strategy that could double sales, cut costs by a third and win industry admiration. Nonetheless, it still affects people. To be successful, how

---

[1] This technique was originally developed by <u>Sakichi Toyoda</u> and was used within the <u>Toyota Motor Corporation</u> during the evolution of its manufacturing methodologies.

people feel has to be figured out and what anxieties or fears the idea might provoke and then factor that into how to frame, socialize and implement the ideas. Organizations don't change; but people do. 'Leadership' does not say yay or nay to an idea; but people do.

Which Relationships Are Especially Important? – The most important part of mastering the organizational landscape is understanding the different types of people who populate it and which relationships are especially important to build. Most of the employees tend to develop relationships with people they like and who are like them and avoid people whose views and mind-sets are really different from theirs.

But when it comes to creating change, one need to develop relationships with people who can help them or stop them. These are primarily about the people who fall into the category of bureaucrats. They are pretty much everyone's favorite people to mock and disparage, but the advice is to invest the energy in better understanding the varying roles that bureaucrats play in organizations. They will even go so far as to suggest that befriending some of these bureaucrats could end up being one of the most useful things rebels can do to improve their chances for success.

Work Politics: Who exactly is a bureaucrat anyway – a bureaucrat is a person who faithfully uses his judgment and skills in service of a higher authority and who "must sacrifice his personal judgment if it runs counter to his official duties."

Some bureaucrats are interested in nudging the organization in the right direction, while others are more concerned with completing their to-do lists on time and on budget or even—gasp—advancing their own careers.

There are four of the most noteworthy types of bureaucrats everyone will encounter;

> ### *Types of Bureaucrats*
> 1. *Bureaucratic Black Belts - BBB*
> 2. *Tugboat Pilots*
> 3. *Benevolent Bureaucrats*
> 4. *Wind Surfers*

Bureaucratic Black Belts - The term bureaucratic black belts (BBBs) is to describe people who have mastered their organization's rules and culture and whose primary motivations appear to be making sure that the organization's rules are followed and operational integrity is maintained.

Tugboat Pilots – Tugboat pilots are often some of the most valuable members of an organization's leadership team because of their ability to navigate difficult organizational terrain, whether congressional hearings, new leadership, bad publicity, or new administrations. Like mountain goats, their first step, their first bureaucratic response, is always spot-on. They can recall every detail of an organization's history and leverage it to their advantage.

They differ from BBBs in that their orientation is not conservative, per se. They are motivated not so much by making sure the organization's rules are followed as by figuring out the best way to get the organization's mission accomplished. They are much less likely than rebels to imagine significant new approaches, because they value expediency, sound tactics and near-term results.

Benevolent Bureaucrats – Benevolent bureaucrats can slow the progress down, but not because they want to stop. These kinder, gentler bureaucrats may calculate that the change idea has a chance of winning support from senior leaders and they want to be associated with the Big Deal in some way. They do not know enough about the initiative to provide substantive value, so they pick on small things.

Wind Surfers – Wind surfers are one of the most difficult personality types rebels will find in the organizational landscape. Wind surfers are BBBs with strong personal ambitions who have mastered the organizational landscape — and every angle to ascend the hierarchy. While they may have held convictions about how the organization could improve early in their careers, over time and usually without conscious awareness, their ambitions overcome their desire to improve the organization's effectiveness.

Of course, they would deny this and insist they are just playing for the right time and opportunity, but the opportunity never seems to come. And in the meantime, their views on what the organization needs to do shift with the prevailing winds of leadership.

Organizational native	What they care about	What they know	Potential as an ally
Bureaucratic black belt	Rules	Secrets and traditions of the organization	Give it a try - medium
Tugboat pilot	Results	How things get done	Highest—Can become a valuable resource
Benevolent bureaucrat	Process	Details, details, details	Low
Wind surfer	Themselves	How to get ahead	Really low

Figure 3 – Types of bureaucrats

Developing Good Relationships – Is the idea especially important to the organization right now? Can it could make a difference? If so, one can make friends with those individuals in the organization who can help make it happen. A good first step is getting to know people as people and giving them an opportunity to get to know. We ask people who take our courses to do this and they say it is one of the most helpful things that they have done at work in quite a while. Set up lunch dates with BBBs so that one can begin to understand them. In these informal relationship-development conversations, try to learn what it is like to be them. Put oneself in their place;

- What are they accountable for?
- What are their motivations?
- What does success look like to them?
- What happens if they make a mistake?

Respect Other Views – As unlikely as it may seem, BBBs and many others in the organization may actually love the way things are and believe the status quo is just as it should be. One of the greatest mistake's rebels can make is failing to understand that many leaders want to preserve what they have because they genuinely believe in it.

Those who oppose ideas for change aren't stupid or acting only out of self-interest. For many, the changes we advocate strike at the very essence of something they believe in deeply. Understanding this will impact the approach. It is less likely to underestimate those who do not support the and much more willing to engage in real conservations with them to identify areas for synergy.

Empathize: What's It Like to Be Them? – Developing genuine empathy for those in the organization with bureaucratic tendencies is foundational for building relationships. Tune into their anxieties. It is obvious that this can be challenging, especially if the organization has been continually foiled by BBBs, but it is essential to getting to know them.

This empathy has to be brought in the conversations, letting people know that one wants to understand their perspective. All people want to be seen and to have people understand what it is like to be them. This is especially true of BBBs, who may have an even more difficult role at work than rebels do. Empathy is likely to ease the tension and will perhaps put BBBs slightly more at ease with others.

As a summary;

- Understand what it is like to be them.
- Empathize.
- Ask for advice.
- Have a goal for every conversation.
- Try to find ways to recognize everyone's value.

> *Understanding the psychology of the employees – Human Resources mainly the CxOs is a primary criterion to decide on the Governance*

Understanding the organizational landscape, build supporters and do the homework to support the ideas, including understanding its risks to the organization.

Have the Organizational Landscape been Mastered? – This makes the life easier in governance. This is the foundation on which the building of Governance can be build. This preparation will make it difficult for others to deny the organizational need for the ideas, to discredit the value of the idea, or to discount the legitimacy.

Understanding the psychology of the employees – Human Resources mainly the CxOs is a primary criterion to decide on the Governance method of that particular organization.

Chapter Summary;

Organizational **landscapes** are composed of a collection of functions which are organized in the organization. They include small-scale function/ department onwards major technological dependency.

One has to understand the phycology of the people before clearly define how to govern the Organization.

As a first step to understand the phycology of the people answers to five whys has to be understood.

Types of Bureaucrats are;

1. Bureaucratic Black Belts – BBB
2. Tugboat Pilots
3. Benevolent Bureaucrats

4. Wind Surfers

Understanding the psychology of the employees – Human Resources mainly the CxOs is a primary criterion to decide on the Governance method of that particular organization.

*****

Globalization & Innovation

One of the main phenomena to which organizations are confronted and that has influenced all aspects of social life of people living in the earth is globalization. Globalization is a multi-facet phenomenon which leads to disappearance of the borders between economic, social, cultural and political relations and shapes a modern relation and communication between nations (within and among countries).

Due to the significance of this in the life, it has been the focus of the attention of scholars so that most of them consider globalization as a factor for development, welfare and integration among nations which lead to the distribution of global benefits among people.

> *Globalization is a multi-facet phenomenon which leads to disappearance of the borders between economic, social, cultural and political relations and shapes a modern relation and communication between nations (within and among countries).*

Despite this perspective, some theorists consider it a discriminative force which makes the poor, poorer and the rich, richer. In their views, many people of developed and advanced counties would benefit of globalization while developing and undeveloped countries would drop behind developed countries due to lack of facilities to compete in this area.

Hence based on this, the proponents of globalization consider it as a positive phenomenon in all respects and the opponents, as usual, consider it as the destructive factor of regional and national cultures due to overcoming the capitalism and the increase in economic and political dimensions. Hence, the consequences of globalization on different aspects of human life and different matters lead to dissolution of interpretations.

First the concept of globalization and its origin have to be reviewed and then for better investigation of this relation, the effect of globalization on different aspects of innovation also has to be analyzed. It is believed that globalization reduces innovation following the reduction of variety in different aspects of the society including economic, social, political and cultural dimensions and inclination toward integration and unification and it has negative effect on innovation.

At the outset, the term 'globalization' has different definitions under the influence of ideological backgrounds of researchers. Some consider globalization the same as communication revolution, others have considered it as a form of post-modernism and some others has regarded it as a new form of states without border. The optimistic view towards this phenomenon has considered it as a factor for growth, peace and friendship and the proximity of nations, also abundance of blessings and the pessimistic view equals it to crisis poverty and the disappearance of weak communities and unequal competition.

From among the provided definitions the globalization has been classified into five groups;

> *Globalization cannot be defined uniquely and has been defined differently by different authors.*

1. The first definition considers globalization synonymous with internationalization assuming that globalization leads to closer relation between nations within the framework of flowing of trade and investment and easier and faster communications. However, this definition has been criticized by some scholars that cross-border relation between nations has existed long before the term 'globalization' entered in international relation dictionary. Based on it, such definition does not provide a convincing meaning of globalization.

2. The second definition considers globalization as de-terrorization and liberalization and describes it as an integration process of international economy and reduction of legal limitation of import and export of goods, services, cash and financial tools. In this view, globalization refers to a movement among nations leading to liberalization of negotiations between them and other nations and creates a borderless space for economic and financial affairs. On the other hand, critics of this definition reject the general identity of the two terms "globalization and liberalization" and argue that this integration process for connecting the nations have also appeared long before, especially at the time when imperial powers of Europe preserved their control on third-world countries.

3. Third definition assumes globalization as universalization; It has been considered as the process of spreading the topics, experiences and values all over the worlds and between people living in the earth. In other words, the universalization informs of the combination of cultures and the experiences of people. In confirmation of samples globalization is referred to as the spreading of TV, automobile and so on and the same trends of life and government of organizations. However, some critics have criticized this definition also that the transcontinental spreading of religions and trades have been long before globalization. Hence the term 'Universality' is proper for describing the spread of experiences and values and it should be confined to new global activities, which have emerged from second half of the 20th century.

4. The fourth definition regards globalization as synonymous with westernization and modernization and considers it as the dynamic factor which mentions the development of modernized social structure (capitalism, rationalism, industrialization, bureaucracy) and destructs non-westernized nations' identities and cultures. As an evidence for globalization Hollywood culture and McDonald fast food

restaurant can be mentioned. The critics of this definition describe the spread of such western values under concepts such as colonization, westernization and modernization. In this area there is no need to create the term 'globalization' for describing western ideas and values in third world countries.

5. The fifth definition is offered as deterritorialization. In this definition the geographical borders disappear and lose their significance. The social space is not defined within the traditional borders and geographical borders change and they would become super-territorial.

The above definitions are among the most common definitions of globalization, each of which view globalization from a different perspective. Although all of them suggest that a governing and organizing method would be created in form of comprehensive globalization which includes all powers which direct the world toward global village, reduce the distances, make convergence in cultures and reduce political borders.

Historically, globalization is not a new phenomenon but its changes can be investigated in terms of scale, speed and cognition. Within scale framework, economic, political and social relation between nations have become more than before. Globalization has experienced a kind of temporal and spatial compression in terms of speed which had not experienced it before. Within the framework of cognition, it considers the globe as a smaller space where every phenomenon and event have some consequences on economic, social and political life.

Anyway, the term globalization has been offered and it becomes a catchword for most scholars from all parts of the world after collapse of Soviet Union and the end of cold war in late 20th century. In the 1970s, this term developed as "Global Village" which reflected the progress of technology which has made the international exchanges and trade easier and faster.

Dimensions of globalization;

It is worth noting that globalization is not a one-dimensional phenomenon. It has different dimensions and it can be divided into several complicated and interrelated dimensions. These dimensions can be examined from different aspects.

One aspect is to view four dimensions of globalization viz.

1. Economic,
2. Political.
3. Social and
4. Cultural.

These four dimensions include different factors such as communications, transportation, technology, population mobility and life style.

Furthermore, the consequence of each factor might be related to more than one dimension. For example, in the first view, it might have economic applications and meanwhile the technology affects the production, employment and the use of standard and life style.

The four dimensions of globalization can also be distinguished as economic, military, cultural and social.

Economic dimension;

In definition of globalization, economic perspective is of great importance and is dominant in contrast to political, scientific, cultural and social dimensions. The reason is the evolution of this dimension of globalization rather than other dimensions and time priority. This is why globalization is viewed mostly from economic point of view. The origin of economy globalization and its development is Breton Woods conference in 1944. However, the economy crisis of the 1970s facilitated globalization through creation of new drivers in neoliberal economic ideology.

On the other hand, advances in technology that reduced the transportation and communication costs reinforced this trend. One of the other significant factors in development of economic globalization is the role of multinational companies and the emergence of networks of companies which act independent of particular geographical areas or state's policies.

This economic dimension is most important in deciding the governance method for an organization since it affects the economic result viz. the profit most.

Political dimension;

Globalization as a political phenomenon means that the construction of political plays is not determined within distinct and independent units (independent organized structures and hierarchy of states). Therefore, that globalization is the process of political structuration. Political globalization is the reconstruction of political experiences and institutionalized structures for coordinating and removing the deficiencies of state.

On the other hand, according to some of theorists, globalization reduces the control of states and governments of their nations. Hence social liberation, democracy, civil attitudes and political culture are promoted.

Cultural dimension;

The effect of globalization of cultural dimension is different and globalization of culture had different reactions. However, the specification and identity of these reactions depend on those societies where it has occurred, in a way that the reaction of western and modern societies has been different from that of developing countries and other countries. Two factors have been effective in this phenomenon – first, the economic and financial effect of globalization and modernity, the emergence of modern consumption goods, the effect of mass media. Second one is western values including scientific argumentation, secularism, individualism, freedom of speech, political pluralism, ruling of law, equalization of women and minorities. Theorists have different view toward the influence of globalization on culture. Proponents believe that although globalization leads to integration and removal of cultural barriers, it is an important step toward more stable world and better life for individuals. However, others consider globalization of culture improper due to fear from universal power and the continuance of multinational collaborations with international institutions such as International Monetary Fund (IMF).

Globalization and innovation;

What has been discussed so far is for better determination of globalization process and the examination of its consequences in different cultural, social, political and economic dimensions. Nevertheless, the main focus is the consequences and effects of globalization on innovation and regardless of the positive and negative effects in different aspects, how globalization affects innovation. The researchers have offered different explanations and analysis about globalization and its consequences. Each of these scholars and theorists has tried to examine different dimensions of this phenomenon. Despite most of them, the overall effect of globalization is to move towards convergence and integration. It is believed that "globalization is the process of shaping some networks within which the societies which were isolated in this world merge in mutual dependency and global unity". The relation between nations a kind of convergence and integration between nations can be considered.

Such theories reflect the orientation of globalization toward integration. However, such integration can have different influences from different dimensions. Economically, the world is being transformed to a unique economic creature very quickly, an undeniable creature within which all components and parts are dependent to one another.

From political and social perspectives, the results of globalization are the construction of transnational society which if it is done on all aspects, the political and cultural role of states is reduced and the transnational rules and values would govern the economic, political, cultural and social structures. Furthermore, from cultural point of view, it leads to universal culture beyond local and national borders, the common and shared culture within the framework of which local cultures are defined and if this culture has the ability to collaborate in such culture, it would stay stable. Based on this, most of the scholars regard globalization as the unification of all cultures and extension of westernized civilization's patterns that is in fact a cultural imperialism.

Considering these consequences of globalization, the main conclusion is that globalization reduces innovation and it has a negative effect on innovation through removing the variation. It is obvious that the consequence of such phenomenon is disappearance of variety in these dimensions. In economic dimension, globalization is an economic phenomenon whose feature is the spread of capitalism and market mechanism all over the world. Since different countries have different social and political systems and their economies are in different level of growth and development, the obligations and necessities of economy globalization (liberation of trade and capital flow), the execution of social regulations (those emerged from global organizations like world trade organization, ...) have different effects on nations. Such discussion in globalization embeds this idea that the prerequisites of globalization destruct variation in all dimensions and due to fact that variation has positive effects on improving innovation and creativity and is considered a source of innovation, globalization phenomenon destructs innovation through destruction of variation and with inclination toward convergence and integration.

In culture dimension, the negative effects of globalization have been considered in eradicating variety. The critics of globalization assert that globalization is somehow imposition of western culture on non- western world. This theory that is mentioned within cultural imperialism follows the idea that although cultural globalization appears as trans-historical and transnational or as a supreme global power, it is nothing more than the issuance of goods, values and priorities of western life style.

Conclusion;

Globalization is one of the topics which have been considered by different theorists and researchers and different contradictory views have been provided considering its significance and influence on various aspects of human life (economic, social, political and cultural).

On one hand, the proponents of globalization try to focus more on the benefits of this phenomenon and emphasize on economic and social development of communities and regards it a positive matter. In contrast, the opponents of globalization believe that globalization is good for developed and advanced countries and communities and it has negative consequences in other communities (developing countries). However, some believe that beyond the identity of societies and communities, globalization has different consequences for topics and phenomena.

The main impact of globalization is the development of technology, science can be positive or negative. The effect of globalization on innovation has some negative consequences on innovation through destruction of variety and with inclination toward convergence in all areas and eliminates variety.

Innovation on account of Globalization has a huge impact on technology, which has directly affected the economic result of business enterprises. To achieve results every organization should understand the impact of globalization and innovation on the industry and hence the Due to the fact that convergence and orientation toward integration occur in all dimensions including economic, social, political and cultural dimensions, in other words, moving in one dimension affects other dimensions, so it can be concluded that the negative effect of globalization on innovation occur in all dimensions.

Chapter Summary;

Globalization is a multi-facet phenomenon which leads to disappearance of the borders between economic, social, cultural and political relations and shapes a modern relation and communication between nations (within and among countries).

Globalization cannot be defined uniquely and has been defined differently by different authors.

IMPORTANCE OF GLOBALIZATION

Innovation on account of Globalization has a huge impact on technology, which has directly affected the economic result of business enterprises. To achieve results every organization should understand the impact of globalization and innovation on the industry and hence the market.

Risk Management

What is Risk? - *"It is better to be approximately right than precisely wrong"*.

The dictionary definition of risk is the chance of disaster or loss. Here, **risk** is defined as the chance of a bad outcome. This implies that risk only relates to situations where a negative outcome could occur and that the likelihood of such an outcome can be estimated.

Risk, in traditional terms, is viewed as a 'negative'. Webster's dictionary, for instance, defines risk as "exposing to danger or hazard".

The Chinese give a much better description of risk as

The first is the symbol for 'danger', while the second is the symbol for 'opportunity', making risk a mix of danger and opportunity.

What is Risk Management? - *"Risk Management is asking what might happen the other 1 percent of the time"*. A *risk* occurs when a chosen action or inaction could lead to a potential loss or undesirable outcome. Therefore, *risk management* is achieved by defining and enforcing processes and a framework to identify risk factors, analyzing and quantifying the impact on organizations' finances and reputation and putting in place methods to mitigate or accept the risk.

> *Risk is part and parcel of any business. It cannot be fully avoided. It can utmost be managed, mitigated and transferred. Even when it is transferred it cannot be fully transferred.*

Enterprise Risk Management is a huge topic on its own and a book of this nature cannot cover it comprehensively. It is attempted to give an idea or overview of the risks and risk management, mainly based for Banks on Basel accords. Basel IV has already started its presence in bits and pieces and the plan is to make it regulatory by 2024. But it is not considered in this book.

Risk Management is not the responsibility of a single person. The suggested risk management governance structure would be;

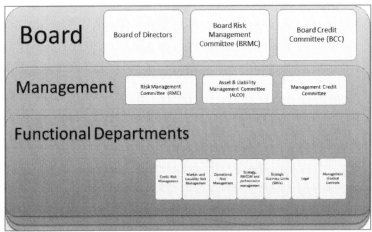

Figure 4 – Risk Governance Structure

The components of a risk can be, at a high level, listed as;

- Threat – Threat describes the source of a risk being realized. Where appropriate to their organization's context, the business should apply the threat profile for OFFICIAL, supplemented if necessary, with local or specific threat intelligence wherever it is available.

- Likelihood – Likelihood also known as 'probability' estimates how likely it is for a threat to occur. It can be captured by examining historical data of compromises to estimate how history will be repeated.
- Impact - Impact describes the consequences of a risk being realized. To allow risk evaluation and prioritization, impact should specify the negative effect that a risk's realization would entail. This should include expected losses (e.g. financial and reputation losses) as well as business objectives which would not be achievable as a result of the impact.

Likelihood of risk occurrences can be classified as;

- RARE: The threat may occur in very exceptional circumstances
- UNLIKELY: The threat could occur sometime in the target period
- POSSIBLE: The threat may occur within the target period
- LIKELY: The threat is likely to occur within the target period
- EXPECTED: The threat is expected to occur within the target period

The treatment of the risks can be as below depending on the above likelihood;

- AVOID – Identified risks can be avoided if alternative technical or business decisions are made on the service design

- MITIGATE – Identified risks can be mitigated if a treatment or control will reduce the impact or likelihood.
- TRANSFER – Identified risks are transferred to more appropriate business areas or responsibility is escalated.
- ACCEPT – Identified risks are accepted in the event that business needs override the impact of the risk or is within the business risk appetite.

The risk management is not a one-time activity. It is a continuous through-life Process. Its life-cycle can be noted as;

- Produce a Risk Status and Management Dashboard, for weekly, monthly or real time reporting.
- Develop and maintain an Audit and Assurance program, to ensure that Service Providers and system Suppliers security assurances are actively audited, validated and managed.
- Plan and schedule Risk Management Checkpoints to ensure that Risk Treatment Plans and security validations are reviewed and assured in a forecastable and pragmatic way.
- Use a Risk Report to document business risk decisions and provide supporting risk and assurance detail with a proportional Digital Risk Management Record Schema.

Risks in BFS Industry

Organizations have to manage a galaxy of risks as depicted in the below figure 2. There is no way that these risks can be avoided. By proper risk management the effect of risks can be minimized, but it can never be avoided. There is one simple way to avoid all these risks – close down the shutters – that means if anyone is any business there will definitely be a risk. Without risk management there is no question of managing an organization.

The major risks faced by organizations can be classified as in the landscape below Figure 3.

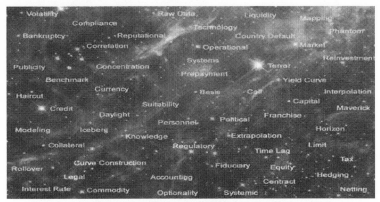

Figure 5 – Galaxy of Risks in Banks

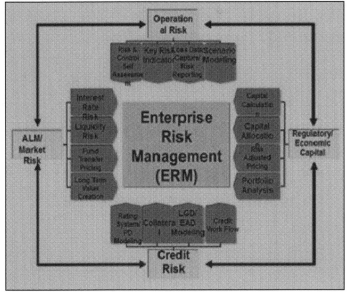

Figure 6 – FI's Risk Landscape

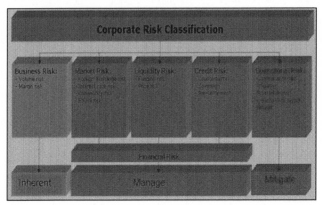

Figure 7 – Classification of Risks

The Risks of an organization can be classified into three viz.;

- Inherent to the business – on account of business (paid to take)
- Due to management/ mis-management (Paid to Manage)
- On account of operations - avoidable/ mitigatable

The treatments for different risks are different.

Some more risk-related terms are important and worth noting;

- **Risk event** is defined as the occurrence of an event that creates the potential for loss (a bad outcome)
- **Risk loss** refers to the losses incurred as a direct or indirect consequence of the risk event. Such losses can be either financial or non-financial.
- **Risk Governance** – Establish and Maintain a Common Risk View, Integrate with Enterprise Risk Management (ERM) and Make Risk-aware Business Decisions

- **Risk Evaluation** – Collect Data, Analyze Risk and Maintain Risk Profile
- **Risk Response** – Articulate Risk, Manage Risk and React to Events
- **Risk Appetite** – the amount of risk an entity is prepared to accept when trying to achieve its objectives. The enterprise's objective capacity to absorb loss (e.g., financial loss, reputation damage).

The (management) culture or predisposition towards risk taking - cautious or aggressive (i.e. what is the amount of loss the enterprise wants to accept to pursue a return?)

- **Risk Tolerance** – the tolerable deviation from the level set by the risk appetite and business objectives. e.g., standards require projects to be completed within estimated budgets and time, but overruns of 10 percent of budget or 20 percent of time are tolerated

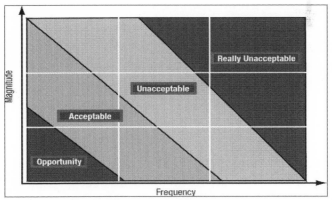

Figure 8 – Classification of Risks

Sources of risks – The sources of risks vary and depend on the type of business. For instance, typically Financial intermediaries have to do the below tasks inherent to the business and have to face the related risks also;

- Hold assets that are potentially subject to default (Credit Risk)
- Tend to mismatch the maturities of their balance sheets' assets and liabilities (Market Risk and/ or Interest Rate Risk)
- Are exposed to saver withdrawal risk depending on the type of claims they have sold to liability holders (Liquidity Risk)
- Are exposed to market risks due to trading activities
- Are exposed to other risks servicing the customers/ transactions (operational, fraud etc.)

Most managers are familiar with the regulation of non-financial products. Many governments set out guidelines or rules that a company must follow in order to get its product to market. For *example*, cars are subject to product regulation, such as the requirement for seatbelts or airbags. The regulation is there to protect customers.

The financial services industry is also subject to regulations to protect customers and increase confidence in its products. Banks, however, are subject to further regulation. Indeed, in the case of banking regulation it is the institution itself that is strictly regulated, not simply the products and services it offers. While it is common to have regulation covering the products or services an industry offers. It is more unusual to have every institution in the industry regulated.

The reason for this high degree of regulation is that the impact of a failure of a bank can have a deep and long-term impact across an entire economy.

While a car manufacturer is subject to product regulation, it is not governed by a regulatory body that regulates every car producer. The car manufacturer may be subject to corporate law and the disclosure requirements of stock exchanges; however, it is free to capitalize itself in whatever way and to whatever extent its management believes is necessary. The company's shareholders provide the only restraint on its management.

This is not the case for banks as they are not free to choose their capital structure. **Capital structure** refers to the way in which a bank finances itself, usually through a combination of equity issues, bonds and loans. The capital structure of a bank is determined by local supervisors who stipulate the minimum capital requirements, as well as the minimum level of liquidity the bank is required to hold and the type and structure of its lending.

If an organization has sufficient capital it has tolerable financial resources to meet potential losses. If it has adequate liquidity it has satisfactory financial resources to fund its assets and to meet its obligations as they fall due.

Capital structure of an organization – Balance Sheet of FI 'A';

Assets	Amount (USD Million)	Risk Weight %	RWA (USD Million)
Domestic government Bonds	100	0	0
Cash	10	0	0
Loans to other banks < 1 year	200	20	40
Loans to MSMEs	390	100	390
Loans to local authorities	200	50	100
Loans to international companies	100	100	100
Total	1,000		630
Liabilities			
Capital	80		
Creditors	820		
Loans from banks	100		
Total	1,000		

Notes:

1. RWA = Risk-Weighted Assets
2. Minimum required capital is 8%
3. FI (Financial Institution) 'A' does not trade in the markets and hence does not have a trading book
4. Ratio of regulatory capital to RWA = 8% of USD 630 million = USD 50.4 million
5. Comparison of required capital to capital held = USD 50.4 million < USD 80 million

This is a much-simplified sample capital structure of a FI. It can be noted that given its asset structure, the supervisor requires the FI to hold minimum capital of USD 50.4 million. The FI is holding USD 80 million, thus surpassing the supervisor's requirement.

Why regulate a FI alone?

The need for FIs to be regulated as institutions has its origins in the risk inherent in the system. Unlike the automobile industry, FIs offer a product that is used by every single commercial and personal customer - money. Thus, the failure of an FI, both partially or totally, can affect the entire economy and is referred to as 'systemic risk'.

Systemic risk is the risk that failure a FI could result in damage to the economy out of all proportion to simply the immediate damage to employees, customers and shareholders. While most people may not be familiar with the term systemic risk, they do understand what is meant by a 'run on a FI'. This occurs when a FI cannot cover its liabilities; i.e. it does not hold enough cash to pay the depositors who wish to withdraw their funds. The inability to meet liabilities and repay depositors does not necessarily have to be real; it can simply be the result of a perception on the part of its customers.

The below can be further more reasons for high degree of regulation of FIs by the regulators;

- Regulated to protect the customer and the economy financial or non-financial.
- The solvency of a FI is a concern for the whole economy

- There is a major relationship between risks and capital
- Organizations need to have adequate capital to cover the risks they run.
- The effect of economic shocks on organization can be minimized through regulation.
- The impact of risk events can only be minimized.

Example – Run on a FI

FI 'A' is rumored (correctly or not) to have made an extraordinary number of bad loans that have led to losses. This rumor causes the FI's depositors to withdraw their deposits. If FI 'A' does not hold enough cash, depositors will be unable to withdraw their money, adding to the concern over the FI's stability. This causes more depositors to attempt to withdraw their deposits. Whether the original problem is real or not, the level of withdrawals means FI 'A' is unable to continue business.

The failure of A causes loans to be foreclosed, as the A no longer has the deposits to fund them. If A is sufficiently large, its closing (or failure) could have a ripple effect through the local economy; however, if it operates globally, the impact would be greater.

The solvency of a FI is a concern not only for its shareholders, customers and employees, but also for those who are in charge of managing the economy as a whole – i.e., for all the stakeholders.

Let us look back at the balance sheet given above. This FI has USD 820 million of deposits from customers but only USD 10 million of cash with which to repay the depositors immediately. To raise more cash, it could sell its government bond holdings and potentially raise a further USD 100 million. Any attempt to raise further funds would result in loans being sold or foreclosed.

Prior to the 1930s, 'runs' on FIs and solvency problems occurred relatively frequently. (The last financial crisis of this nature occurred in the US in 1933 and in the UK in 1957). These led governments to control FIs through regulation, ensuring that they were well capitalized and reasonably liquid. Supervisors (usually central FIs) sought to ensure that FIs could:

- Meet the reasonable level of demand for depositors to be repaid without the need to foreclose on loans
- Sustain a reasonable level of losses as a result of poor lending or cyclical reductions in economic activity, i.e. survive a recession.

The level of capitalization and liquidity were at first fairly arbitrary, with capital often related to some percentage of loans. In setting the amount of capital as a percentage of some types of loans, it became obvious that there was a 'missing link' in calculating the appropriate capital level for a FI. This missing link is described using the following *examples*;

FI 'A' only lends to its domestic government and can always assume that the loans will be repaid. FI 'B' only lends to new businesses. It cannot make the same assumption as FI 'A' as some, possibly many, new businesses might fail.

Clearly the economics of lending to the two groups in the *example* above would be a balance between what could be charged for the loans, commonly referred to as the 'margin' and the losses that would be incurred. Any potential investor in A or B is making a risk/ reward decision based on how much risk each FI is willing to take verses how much reward does it wish to gain. In the *example* above B would seek to earn a higher margin than A as it would incur higher losses.

In the case of B, bad debts would unlikely occur at a constant rate as more businesses would default in a recession rather than during periods of economic growth. A bad debt occurs when a FI is unable to recover any of the principal lent to a customer or accrued interest owed. This would cause the FI to suffer variable losses and an erosion of its capital as it is forced to cover each of these losses.

To maintain the expectation that it can survive bad debts, a FI will hold a certain level of funds (capital) from which it would deduct such losses. In the example B would need to hold significantly more capital than A. This is because A pursues a lending policy that, although less rewarding in terms of margin, is more conservative and carries less risk.

From the above *example* it can be seen that the 'missing link' in calculating the appropriate capital level for a FI is the amount of risk it is carrying.

Economic shocks and systemic risk

Despite the best efforts of FIs to ensure diversification of their lending portfolios, many still remain heavily exposed to the economic risks of their home market. The economy of a country can be greatly affected by:

- An external shock, be it a natural disaster or a man-made event and/ or
- Economic mismanagement.

FIs exposed to such an economy may suffer a significant increase in the number of customers defaulting. The increase in the default rate can be attributed to such things as:

- The credit standing of companies affected by the rapid deterioration of the economy
- A significant rise in unemployment levels
- An increase in interest rates.

Many FIs will have difficulty in safeguarding themselves from economic shocks in a specific country. However, there are certain actions they can take to mitigate the economic effects, including:

- Complying with regulation (Basel) which increasingly requires FIs to create economic shock scenarios and ensure they hold sufficient capital to protect stakeholders from the effects of such shocks
- Estimating the resulting levels of bad debts and ensuring their businesses are capitalized accordingly.

Risk and capital

The above *example*s clearly demonstrate the relationship between risk and capital. The more risks a business runs the more capital it requires. FIs are required to hold sufficient capital to cover the risks they run. This is known as **capital adequacy**.

It has also become increasingly clear to supervisors that the level of a FI's capital and its ability to support losses from its lending and other activities should be related to the risks of the business it undertakes, i.e. the level of capital should be based on the level of risk (risk-based capital).

The growth of international BFS markets in the 1970s and 1980s led to the first significant move in the direction of risk-based capital. Thanks in part to the huge increase in oil prices, countries with large US dollar surpluses needed to recycle those dollars to countries with significant deficits. The result was a dramatic growth in international banking and increased competition. It had become clear to supervisors that international FIs needed to ensure they were capitalized against the risks they were running. At the same time lending increasingly took the form of syndicated loan transactions to multinational companies, developing countries and major development projects, all of which represented new areas of lending for many of the FIs involved.

Bank Regulation

Basel I – The Basel Committee on Banking Supervision made the first attempt to establish a standardized methodology for calculating the amount of risk-based capital a FI would be required to hold when it published the first Basel Capital Accord in 1988.

The first Accord only covered credit risk and the relationship between risk and capital was crude by current standards. A simple set of different multipliers (known as risk weights) for government debt, bank debt and corporate and personal debt was multiplied by an overall 8% target capital ratio.

The Market Risk Amendment

Supervisors in several countries extended the 1988 Accord to make it more risk sensitive. Supervisors then moved quickly to take advantage of the work being undertaken by many FIs to manage the risks in their own dealing (trading) operations.

For *example*, to ensure that risks were controlled and priced correctly FIs started setting internal capital requirements for their trading desks. The capital requirements were directly related to the risks that the trading desks were running. To do this the FIs had to establish a view of the relationship between risk and capital. This view was based on the growing use of finance theory, specifically the historic variability of return from different businesses.

The work undertaken by the FIs themselves to manage risks had been given a great deal of impetus as a result of:

- The growth of derivatives markets
- Option pricing models which directly linked the volatility of returns of an underlying market instrument to its price, i.e. risk-based pricing.

The Basel Committee published the Market Risk Amendment to the original Accord in 1996. In addition to creating a simple set of rules for calculating market risk, the Basel Committee encouraged supervisors to focus on appraising the model's FIs used in risk-based pricing. These are the Value at Risk models (Vary).

Basel II - Following the publication of the Market Risk Amendment the Basel Committee began developing a new Capital Accord which was called Basel II. After much consultation and debate the new Accord was adopted in 2004 and is due for implementation. Basel II links the capital of FIs directly to the risks they carry. **Basel II** is an international business standard that requires financial institutions to maintain enough cash reserves to cover risks incurred by operations. The **Basel** accords are a series of recommend-dations on banking laws and regulations issued by the **Basel** Committee on Banking Supervision (BSBS).

The coverage of market risk in Basel II is substantially unchanged from the 1996 Amendment and its subsequent revisions.

At the same time the coverage of credit risk mirrors, to some extent, the Market Risk Amendment. FIs are encouraged to adopt a model-based approach to credit risk pricing and supervisors are encouraged to appraise these models.

Operational risk is included for the first time and, as with credit risk, a model approach is encouraged, although recognition is given to the lack of industry consensus over the structure of these models.

The Basel II Accord also has provisions for other risks to be taken into account when calculating the risk-based capital of a FI; however, these are not covered by a model approach.

Local supervisors will be responsible for implementing Basel II in accordance with their own laws and regulations. The consistent implementation of the new Framework across borders, through enhanced supervision and cooperation, is crucial. Consistent implementation will also be important to avoid confusion over dual reporting to 'home' (where the FI is legally established) and 'host' (where the FI may have branches or subsidiaries) country supervisors.

> *The Basel Accords are four series of banking regulations (Basel I, II, III and IV) set by the Basel Committee on Bank Supervision (BCBS). The committee provides recommendations on banking regulations, specifically, concerning capital risk, market risk and operational risk. The accords ensure that financial institutions have enough capital on account to absorb unexpected losses.*

Effects on supervisors and regulation;

Developments in the financial markets and liberalization of cross-border controls led supervisors and especially central FIs, to consider that although the value of the safety net provided by their lender of last resort function had grown substantially the basis of much of their financial regulation had been weakened.

Prior to the period of financial liberalization in the 1970s and 1980s financial regulation had focused on:

- The authorization of financial institutions

- Tightly defining the spheres of permitted activity of different financial institutions
- The definition of balance sheet ratios and requirements such as keeping a certain level of cash deposits with the regulator, or keeping a certain level of assets in domestic government securities.

New approaches to regulation

In this 'new' world prudential supervisors began to look at potential new approaches to regulation, drawing the following conclusions:

- Significant market participants measured their own performance by looking at the return on the risks they took. If the supervisors could create regulatory processes that worked with the markets, they could make regulation both more effective and more relevant to the regulated institutions
- The increase in the globalization of capital markets greatly increased the need to ensure prudential norms were accepted internationally and implemented consistently
- Regulation was only one part of the solution. The risks of financial intermediation, internationally, depended on such issues as ensuring minimum standards in contract and bankruptcy law, accounting and audit standards and disclosure requirements.

Earlier a galaxy of risks was just indicated through a diagram. Some of them are defined here at least for academic interest;

Market risk – the risk of losses in on- and off-balance sheet positions arising from movements in market prices. It is a group of risks that stem from changes in interest rates, foreign exchange rates and other market determined prices such as those for equities and commodities.

Credit risk – the risk of losses associated with the possibility that the counterparty will fail to meet the obligations; or in simple terms it is the risk that a borrower will not repay what is owed.

Example – a FI lends mortgages to its customers. In doing so it runs the risk that some or all of its customers will fail to pay either the interest or the original sum borrowed.

Operational risk – the risk of loss resulting from inadequate or failed internal processes, people and systems, or from external events.

Opportunity risk – It is a type of risk people often assume unknowingly when they are attempting to avoid risk in general. Sitting on the sidelines or placing your money under the mattress can seem safe.

Default risk – is the chance that a company or individual will be unable to make the required payments on their debt obligation. Lenders and investors are exposed to default risk in virtually all forms of credit extensions. A higher level of risk leads to a higher required return and in turn, a higher interest rate

Strategic risk is the risk associated with the long-term business decisions made by the management.

Systemic risk is the possibility that an event at the company level could trigger severe instability or collapse an entire industry or economy. Systemic risk was a major contributor to the financial crisis of 2008. Companies considered to be a systemic risk are called "too big to fail".

Systematic risk is inherent to the entire market or market segment. Systematic risk, also known as "undiversifiable risk," "volatility" or "market risk," affects the overall market, not just a particular stock or industry. This type of risk is both unpredictable and impossible to completely avoid.

Longevity risk – One of the greatest concerns the investors have is that they will outlive their money. This is longevity risk in a nutshell.

Inflation risk – Inflation is the increase in the cost of goods and services in an economy relative to the currency. When we experience inflation in the United States, the same number of dollars will buy less in the market that it did in the past.

Sovereign risk is the chance that a regulator will implement foreign exchange rules that will significantly reduce or negate the worth of its forex contracts. It also includes the risk that a foreign nation will either fail to meet debt repayments or not honor sovereign debt payments.

Business risk – relates to the competitive position of an organization and the likelihood of it prospering in changing markets.

Business Risk is the chance that the resources expended to implement the change will turn out to have been wasted. Will that change actually produce the expected benefits with no unexpected collateral damage?

Failure to gain the desired business outcome could be caused by a number of factors, principal;

- Choosing the wrong fix for the wrong problem at the wrong time
- Not having a clear line-of-sight from the change to business value
- Lack of alignment between the fix and the organization itself.

Organizational Risk – Organizational Risk is the chance the organization will not fully engage with the new approach or, in some documented cases, simply ignore it and stick to the old ways.

Failure to use the new system could be caused by a number of factors – one of the most common and deadly factors is "workforce resistance".

The primary approach to mitigating Organizational Risk is the systematic and comprehensive use of Change Management to ensure that the organization will be positioned to engage with the change after technical installation.

Change Management is the body of knowledge that is used to ensure that a complex change, like that associated with a big new IT system or a corporate reengineering initiative, gets the right results, in the right timeframe at the right costs. It is a disciplined approach applied in the organizational units that will be affected by the change to ensure their acceptance and readiness to operate effectively in alignment with what is supposed to be the "new reality".

Technical Risk – Organizations, their vendors and service providers have been doing high quality Risk Management for a couple of decades.

Most of the risks that could be managed, however, are limited to the technical/ mechanical risks of the implementation project.

The best layman's definition of the technical risk is associated with the critical questions – will the system/ process/ organization work, will it work on time and will it come in on budget?

This kind of technical risk, while occasionally mismanaged, is usually handled quite well by a combination of the organization's subject matter experts and the vendors.

Reputational risk – is not just limited to the reputation of an organization; it encompasses the whole industry. Quantifying the loss resulting from reputational risk can be difficult given the long-term and widespread nature of the effects.

Chapter Summary

The BFS industry is different from other industries in that the failure of a FI, either partial or total, will have an impact on the entire economy; hence FI failure carries 'systemic risk'.

FIs as financial intermediaries are a powerful force for allocating loan capital to enterprises and thus 'employing' the savings of their depositors. If, however, a FI made loans that borrowers could not repay, the insolvency of the FI could lead not only to the destruction of shareholders' equity but to the destruction of depositors' funds as well. This is because a FI is, by its very nature, highly geared.
On account of inherent nature of its business, FIs do face a galaxy of risks out of which Credit, Operational and Market Risks are the major ones.

Depending on its size and risk appetite FIs do take various management systems. But the maxim is that "Risks cannot be avoided – at the most their impact can be reduced by proper management".

The Basel Accords are four series of banking regulations (Basel I, II, III and IV) set by the Basel Committee on Bank Supervision (BCBS). The committee provides recommendations on banking regulations, specifically, concerning capital risk, market risk and operational risk. The accords ensure that financial institutions have enough capital on account to absorb unexpected losses.

Basel II is an international business standard that requires financial institutions to maintain enough cash reserves to cover risks incurred by operations. The Basel accords are a series of recommendations on banking laws and regulations issued by the Basel Committee on Banking Supervision (BSBS).

The key difference between the Basel II and Basel III are that in comparison to Basel II framework, the Basel III framework prescribes more of common equity, creation of capital buffer, introduction of Leverage Ratio, Introduction of Liquidity coverage Ratio (LCR) and Net Stable Funding Ratio (NSFR).

In December 2017 the Basel Committee on Banking Supervision (BCBS) published a package of proposed reforms for the global regulatory framework of our industry which is frequently referred to as 'Basel IV'. The Committee's aim is to make the capital framework more robust and to improve confidence in the system.

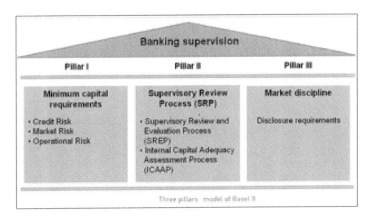

Figure 9 – Three pillars of Basel

*****

Financial Risk

There are few main types of financial risks in addition to what was earlier mentioned as Credit Risk etc.;

> *Financial Risk is a conglomeration of various risks like but not limited to*
> - *Interest Rate Risk*
> - *Exchange Risk*
> - *Commodity Risk*
> - *Price Risk*
> - *Soverign Risk*
> - *Political Risk*
> - *Liquidity Risk*
> - *Operational Risk*
>
> *These are part of Market Risk category.*

Interest Rate Risk

Changes in interest rates lead to a reduction of the value of bonds. Bonds that pay out more interest than current market rates fetch more value than the ones that offer less. Interest rate fluctuations affect the value of the bonds; for example, the value of a bond issued at a 2% rate will increase if the market interest rate falls below 2% because this bond will fetch more return when compared to the market.

Exchange rate or currency risk

Companies transacting across borders using different currencies are exposed to exchange rate or currency risk. Companies are exposed to this risk if they invest or trade goods and services that require payments/ receipts in currencies other than the companies' operating currency. For example, the value of a $1,000 investment made in euros at a rate of $1 = 0.85 EUR will be 850 EUR. If the dollar strengthens to $1 = 0.95 EUR, even when the original investment did not change from $1,000, the exchange rate leads to a devalued original investment of $895.

Commodity risk

The prices of commodities—such as crude oil, copper, or corn that are key to determine the cost of product—change in such a way that a profit margin is diminished, thereby adversely affecting company's profitability.

Price risk

The price of stocks or bonds in a financial market might change due to the specific performance of a company or industry. For example, a change in global crude oil rates has a direct impact on oil company stock prices.

Other risks

Market risk categories in addition to the ones just mentioned include (but aren't limited to) the following;

- Inflation risk: Increase in price of goods and services reduces the value of money as well as the value of investments.
- Country risk or Sovereign Risk: Change in government policies in a foreign country can adversely affect the investment made in that country.
- Political/ social risk; Response of the market to social and political events such as war, election, political instability and changes in policy decisions can lead to market disruptions.
- Liquidity risk; Ability to mobilize liquid cash to meet organizational obligations or to materialize on investment opportunity.
- Operational risk; Risk arising due to the operations of an organization. This risk is caused by internal factors

such as policies, employee errors and IT system failures.

Risk Mitigation

Risk mitigation is the process of minimizing the impact of risk. Risk mitigation process can be broken down into the following steps;

1.   Define the risk.

An Organizational Policy has to be established around identifying and mitigating risks.

Depending on the volume of business and possibility of loss due to risk, certain risk exposures can be ignored, whereas some other exposures may be weighted at a higher level (e.g., risk associated with stable forex rates may be dealt with as lower priority than the currencies with high instability).

A risk mitigation and hedging policy has to be created. Risk mitigation comes with a cost and every organization has a different aptitude to absorb risk. Therefore, each organization will define its own policies around what percentage of exposure should be hedged and mitigated.

2.   Measure risks.

Risk Exposure has to be evaluated, quantified and analyzed for its financial impact.

3.   Identify exposures.

Exposure management provides the option to collect data about future cash flows (inflow/ outflow) associated with risk categories that are required to be assessed and mitigated (e.g., vendor invoices to be paid in non-functional currency that could not be affected by foreign exchange [forex] rate fluctuations).

4. Use risk analyzers provided different software applications.

The Market Risk Analyzer and Credit Risk Analyzer are a set of methods to measure risk, evaluate payment flows and simulate market and credit scenarios to assess their impact on the cash flows.

5. Manage the risk.

Enter into deals with financial institutions to hedge the risk using hedge management and hedge accounting. The market risk can be mitigated by hedging according to the tolerance levels defined by an organization's risk mitigation policy and credit risk can be mitigated by establishing credit limits and dynamically evaluating the limits based on changes on credit ratings for the business partner.

Chapter Summary

Financial Risk is not a single risk. It is a conglomeration of various risks like

- Interest Rate Risk
- Exchange Risk
- Commodity Risk
- Price Risk

- Sovereign Risk
- Political Risk
- Liquidity Risk
- Operational Risk

The above, other than the Operational Risk can be categorized as Market Risk and can be called as sub-risks of Market risks. The above list is not comprehensive.

Also, the Financial Risk is not only for FIs, but applicable to most of the industries/ organizations.

Further Financial Risk Management areas can be discussed under Governance Chapter

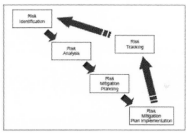

Figure 10 – Stages of Risk Management

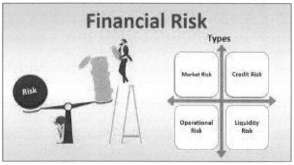

Figure 11 – Major types of Financial Risk

IAS 9 of IFRS

IAS 9 is the International Accounting Standards Board's accounting regulation pertaining to accounting for financial instruments and hedge accounting. Depending on their home country, companies will need to align with IFRS 9 reporting guidelines.

The high-level IAS 9 updates that required reengineering the change in hedge accounting solution are;

- Hedge management can be performed at the net or gross level for exposures. Therefore, a change is needed in SAP to first capture the exposures at the net or gross level and then perform hedge accounting on them at different levels. The hedging area is designed to capture both the exposures; thus, hedge accounting can be done depending on the designation. (Currently, the desig- nation is possible only at the gross level even if net and gross are chosen.)
- A change in the category of exposure item results in the transition of a long-term hedge into a short-term hedge.

*****

IT Risk

Now-a-days every business or organization has started using Information Technology or Information Security (IS) Risk. In fact, most of the organizations, especially FIs depend on IT for its day-to-day operations itself. If there is a failure in systems, then the entire business is stopped. Hence IT risk is more inherent to most of the organizations.

In the present days every organization depend on systems. The dependency is increasing to automate the monotonous activities. Technology risk is also increasing proportionate to the dependency on systems. Earlier this risk was included in Operational Risk and since its dependency and impact have been increasing, this is treated as a separate important risk.

IT Risk also called as Technology Risk. Technology risk also arises from the use of computer systems in the day-to-day conduct of the FI's operations, reconciliation of books of accounts and storage and retrieval of information and reports. The risk can occur due to the choice of faulty or unsuitable technology and adoption of untried or obsolete technology. Major risk arises from breaches of security for access to the computer system, tampering with the system and unauthorized use of it. It is any potential for technology failures to disrupt any business such as information security incidents or service outages.

Historically, information technology was used as a supporting tool for fast and accurate delivery of financial services. Over the years, the uses of information technology in financial services have substantially widened. Fierce competition among banks induced them to enlarge their network of banking products and services and compelled them to offer services off-site and allow the customers to access the computers from their end. Banks are facing greater threats from rapid changes occurring in the technological systems applicable to financial services.

The Risk is more in E-Banking – The introduction of Internet banking service, mobile banking service, Automated Teller Machine (ATM) service and other utility services has increased the information technology risk manifold. The need for providing multiple electronic banking services has pushed banks to bring changes in products and speed up service delivery. The market competition leaves no time for FIs to adjust to.

Information security risk comprises the impacts to an organization and its stakeholders that could occur due to the threats and vulnerabilities associated with the operation and use of information systems and the environments in which those systems operate.

IT Risk is so important because;

- Information is created
- Information is stored and used
- Information is destroyed
- Technology creates opportunities
- Business, education, government, sales of real and electronic goods, e-health, etc.
- IT plays an essential role in these activities. Part of its duty is to protect these information assets

Actually, IT risk can be considered as a business risk, since the business is dependent on IT and on account of;

- Email passwords may be disclosed
- Social network accounts may be used by someone else
- Credit card information may be disclosed
- Customer information may be stolen
- IT service delivery to customers may be poor
- IT systems may be obsolete
- IT projects may be late or fail
- IT systems do not provide any business benefit
- Risk of non-compliance with the regulator
- Own people may harm the systems
- No organization is unaffected
- Businesses are disrupted
- Privacy is violated
- Organizations suffer direct financial loss
- Reputation is damaged

Figure 12 – Effects of IT Risk

Some IT risk related statistics are worth noting here;

- 87% of small business and 93% of larger organizations experienced a security breach in the last year alone
- 85% of breaches took weeks to discover
- 96% of breaches were not highly difficult
- 97% of breaches were avoidable through simple or intermediate controls
- 57% of EU incidents were caused by administrative error, missing hardware, exposed online, or stolen by insiders

IT Risk Management

IT Risk management is the process of identifying areas of risk that could negatively impact the success of the project and proactively managing those areas. Risk assessments are the means used to analyze risk.

Figure 13 – Risk Management Organization

Information security risk management is the systematic application of management policies, procedures and practices to the task of establishing the context, identifying, analyzing, evaluating, treating, monitoring and communicating information security risks.

Information Security Management can be successfully implemented with an effective information security risk management process. There are a number of national and international standards that specify risk approaches and the Forensic Laboratory is able to choose which it wishes to adopt, though ISO 27001 is the preferred standard and the Forensic Laboratory will want to be Certified to this standard.

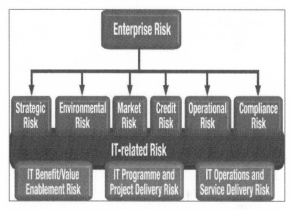

Figure 14 – IT Risk within Enterprise Risk

An IT risk management is not the responsibility of the management. It is an organizational responsibility – Risk management decisions should be objective and informed by an understanding of risk. They should not be made in isolation but on a basis of understanding how individual decisions affect the wider business and what it is trying to achieve.

Tech to deliver business attracts the risk – Organizations should decide for themselves what risk management decisions need to be made to support the delivery and operation of a system or service.

Decisions are to be made by right people, time & support – They need to be empowered by the organization and have the right business, technology, security knowledge and skills to enable informed and objective decisions.

An ISMS is a documented system that describes the information assets to be protected, the Forensic Laboratory's approach to risk management, the control objectives and controls and the degree of assurance required. The ISMS can be applied to a specific system, components of a system, or the Forensic Laboratory as a whole.

As mentioned earlier, risks cannot be avoided. At the maximum its impact can be reduced or minimized.

The process includes 7 steps to minimize technological risks, similar to managing any other risks;

1. Identify key risks, measure probability and impact
2. Analyze security threats.
3. Analyze risk of hardware and software failure.
4. Analyze outsourcing risks.
5. Identify controlled technology.
6. Measuring impact.
7. Rank potential risks and specify desired outcomes.

Cyber-crime has taken on such substantial importance in recent years that target organizations for this information network sensor based iGRC software are likely to be those supporting critical national infrastructure, e.g. verticals and industries with significant brand/ reputation risk. It is suggested that the primary value proposition for iGRC is as follows:

- To provide an insurance policy for CEOs wanting to assure the integrity of critical controls and measures to maintain low probability of occurrence of high impact risk events
- Calibration of risk profiles in the round and validation of controls and measures baselines
- Automatization capabilities of control status and threat level change

The combined involvement in governance, risk and compliance of a wide range of information network sensors is the compelling facet of this now broadened term, integrated governance, risk and compliance. Typical sensor types include:

- Host based intrusion detection, vulnerability assessment, configuration and policy compliance, database logs, web site logs, file accesses
- Hosts for penetration testing, email scanning, spam filters
- Network intrusion detection and prevention, net flow, firewall/ router/ other network devices logs
- Access and identity for successful or failed logins, new users, deleted users, privilege escalation, bio-metric identities
- Web site vulnerability detection (cross site scripting, SQL injection etc.), pages visited, referred from end-point monitoring such as permitted user activity, not permitted user activity, data leakage monitoring, USB usage monitoring and reporting anti-virus, anti-phishing, malware detection applications — most keep

audit logs of activity and others such as event and audit log collection for operating systems, infrastructure and applications

Chapter Summary

IT Risk or Technology Risk or IS Risk are more or less same. Or at least the management of all these risks require same processes.

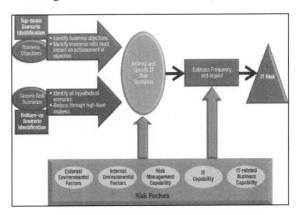

Figure 15 – IT Scenario development

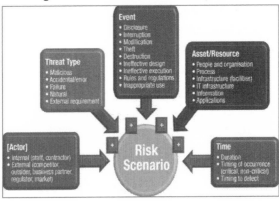

Figure 16 – IT Scenario development - 2

In the present days every organization depend on systems. The dependency is increasing to automate the monotonous activities. Technology risk is also increasing proportionate to the dependency on systems. Earlier this risk was included in Operational Risk and since its dependency and impact have been increasing, this is treated as a separate important risk.

*****

Vendor Risk

When other risks are combined and discussed in a single chapter, Vendor risk is discussed in a separate chapter. This indicates the importance of this risk. Since every business depend on vendors. For instance, a large bank 'ABC' uses the core banking solution of an IT vendor 'XYZ'. Assuming the XYZ company is closed today. What will happen to the bank ABC? Its day-to-day operations will come to a stand-still. This is exactly a major case of Vendor Risk.

A Vendor can be defined as a person or company offering something for sale, including a trader in the street. On the other hand, the buyer is a vendor for the seller and the seller is a vendor for the buyer/

Vendor risk can be defined as a type of operational risk and refers to the risks associated with outsourcing products and/ or services to a third-party.

There are five key drivers of vendor risk;

- Inherent sourcing risk (nature of services/ goods provided)
- Due diligence used in vendor selection
- Contracting form utilized and deviation processes
- Performance measurement, monitoring, & corrective action
- Maturity and effectiveness of vendor's internal policies, procedures and processes

Why is Vendor Risk Management?

It has become a compelling priority to institutions. Focus has shifted from hazard risk to enterprise risk management. Penalties are associated with compliance risks and ever-changing nature of outsourcing.

The real value is in the operational and financial data, the interpretation of the data and the business process that takes that knowledge and drives action. Outcome of a strong vendor risk management programs would be;

- Better sourcing decisions
- Increased risk awareness
- Alignment of vendor management strategy with risk exposure
- Deeper understanding of vendors' operations
- Damage to property
- Physical harm or death
- Financial harm
- Reputational damage
- Liability for acts or omissions of vendor

Vendor Risk Management;

Vendor risk management is a formal way to evaluate, track and measure third-party risk. To assess its impact on all aspects of your business and to develop compensating controls or other forms of mitigation to lessen the impact on your business if something should happen.

Best in class institutions segment their vendors by risk exposure and focus on the small percentage of the overall vendor base that may present a serious risk to the institution.

Goal of risk exposure framework is to create a quick, easy to use process for University internal customers to select vendors for a "deeper dive" risk identification and assessment process.

A vendor risk intelligence system can be created from the compilation of three types of information and data;

- Supplier provided data and information
- Internal customer data and feedback
- Third party resources

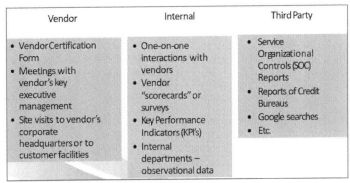

Figure 17 – Vendor Risk Management Components

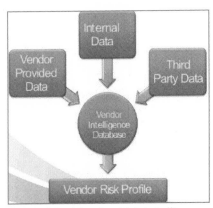

Figure 18 – Vendor Risk Intelligence

Real time vendor risk assessment is ongoing facilitated by:

- Creating a vendor risk intelligence data base that facilitates continual entry of 'leading' risk indicators
- Building vendor risk management (assessment and mitigation) into key procurement processes
- Three Key Areas;
  - Supplier Certification Process
  - RFX Process
  - Contracting
- Appraising the vendors as a credit appraisal
- The concept of 'L1' is gone. Technical knowledge is important.
- Contracting – four critical concerns;
  - Contract Form
  - Contracting Process
  - Risky Provisions
  - Contract Management

Chapter Summary

Since every business depend on vendors, the vendor risk also becomes more important to be managed.
A Vendor is a person or company offering something for sale. Vendor risk is a type of operational risk and refers to the risks associated with outsourcing products and/ or services to a third-party.

Vendor risk has become a compelling priority to institutions. Vendor risk management is a formal way to evaluate, track and measure third-party risk.

*****

Compliance Management

The third component of GRC is Compliance. In general, it means conforming to a rule, such as a specification, policy, standard or law. Regulatory compliance describes the goal that organizations aspire to achieve in their efforts to ensure that they are aware of and take steps to comply with relevant laws, policies and regulations.

Compliance, in simple terms can be understood as – conforming with stated requirements.

At an organizational level, it is achieved through management processes which identify the applicable requirements (defined for example in laws, regulations, contracts, strategies, policies, etc.), assess the state of compliance, assess the risks and potential costs of non-compliance against the projected expenses to achieve compliance

Hence prioritize, fund and initiate any corrective actions deemed necessary. The specification, policy, standard or law to comply with may vary industry to industry, organization to organization. But no business entity can escape from 100% compliance. There could be failure in risk management, but no exception from compliance. Most of the times non-compliance may result in withdrawal of license itself.

For example, with respect to IT compliance regulations like HIPAA and SOX, or standards like PCI-DSS or ISO:27001, outline very specific security criteria that a business must meet to be deemed compliant. Another example of compliance is, when a financial report is prepared that adheres to standard accounting principles like IFRS. Are we really compliant with all necessary regulations? A million-dollar question. Even different audits cannot guarantee.

Are Corporate Compliances considered as just another burdensome, complicated, back office operations and monotonous work? Or can it be seen as any opportunity in it? The opportunity lies in Good Corporate Governance, where disclosure accompanies transparency. Only the culture of strict adherence to good compliance can keep a company ahead on sustainable basis, bring in larger profits.

Enforcing compliance helps the organizations prevent and detect violations of rules, which protects the organization from fines and lawsuits. The compliance process should be ongoing. Many organizations establish a program to consistently and accurately govern their compliance policies over time. There should be specific officer exclusively responsible for compliance areas.

The role of a compliance officer, sometimes also called as compliance manager, is to ensure that an organization is conducting its business in full compliance with all national and international laws and regulations that pertain to the particular industry, as well as professional standards, accepted business practices.

Non-Compliance itself is a Risk. This risk can be classified into six major types;

- Environmental Risk - Potential for damage to living organisms or the environment arising out of an organization's activities.
- Workplace Health & Safety.
- Corrupt Practices.
- Social Responsibility.
- Quality.
- Process Risk.

It is the not management alone to be compliant, but it is the organization as a whole. That means every employee - from security at the gate onwards till CxOs. Even if one employee is non-compliant then the entire organization is.

The elements of a typical Compliance Program can be listed as:

- Implementing written policies, procedures and standards to follow. Also, these policies procedures and standards should be periodically updated and more importantly should be made known to every employee to follow. Conducting effective training and education.
- Designating a compliance officer and compliance committee. The committee must have at least one director level representative.
- Enforcing compliance helps the organization prevent and detect violations of rules, which protects the business from penalties and lawsuits. The compliance process should be ongoing. Many organizations establish a program to consistently and accurately govern their compliance policies over time. Compliance Demands Grow with Business. In its

business sense, 'compliance' refers to a company meeting its legal obligations, often to protect the health, safety and welfare of others.

The benefits of being compliant can be at a high level;

- Reduced Legal Problems.
- Improved Operations and Safety.
- Better Public Relations.
- Higher Employee Retention.

How to achieve compliance? There is no thumb rule across organizations. However, the following steps can be used as a guideline.

- Automate – there are some automation tools wherein the policy, procedure and standards can be converted rules to be automated. Of course, to be keep on updated.
- Periodically meet with the divisional leaders to ensure the policies and procedures are feasible.
- Determine the best format of policies for the organization based on the industry standards.
- Make Policies and Procedures easily accessible to the employees.
- Set deadlines for each policy and procedure to be acknowledged.

The compliance operations professional designs, develops, implements and evaluates the compliance program and monitors its operational implementation. The compliance operations professional also revises the compliance program in response to the changing operational needs of the organization.

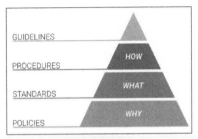

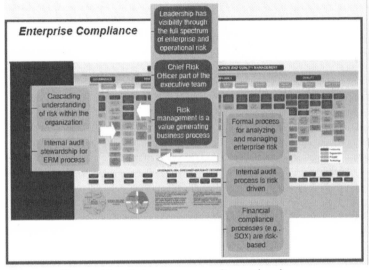

Figure 19 – Enterprise compliance landscape

A compliance management system is an integrated system comprised of written documents, functions, processes, controls and tools that help an organization comply with legal requirements and minimize harm to consumers due to violations of law. The compliance department as a FI's internal police force. It is the unit that ensures that a financial institution complies with applicable laws, regulations and rules and it plays an essential role in helping to preserve the integrity and reputation of the organization.

Clause 49 of Listing Agreement with stock exchanges state that "The Board shall periodically review compliance reports of all laws applicable to the company, prepared by the company as well as steps taken by the company to rectify instances of non-compliances".

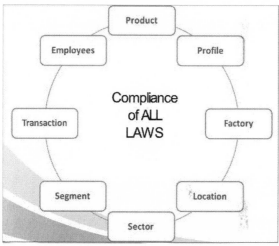

Figure 20 – Compliance of all Laws

The Company Secretary is primarily responsible to coordinate with COMPLIANCE OF ALL LAWS, but the organization is ANSWERABLE.

Corporate Compliance Management is to enhance Value through Governance Systematic - Well Organized Process of Compliant – Compliance Helps in Valued - Build Value. Time has come that Corporate compliance is not merely a legal compliance but it is a NECESSITY.

Corporate Compliance Management is a Five Step Process;

1. Understanding the Organization

   - Organization's History & Background
   - Capital Structure & Evolution
   - Promoters & Group Companies
   - Management & Administration buildup
   - Financial Soundness & Debt Structure
   - Risk Management & Protection
   - Licenses & Approvals

2. Identification

   - General application of laws
   - Sectoral applications
   - Industry/ Segment applications
   - Geographical applications
   - Number of Employees
   - Transaction applications

3. Evaluation

   - Through Questionnaires
   - Evaluating the applicable laws after due identification process

4. Assessment

   - As for instance, A Company has its operations of exports which further Involve lots of foreign exchange transactions.
   - Further improvements

- Implication of Compliance System
- Effective Usability
- Bridging the gap between Compliance in Letter & Compliance in Letter & Spirit
- Identify the gap between the present compliance system and the results of evaluation process

5. Creating a Compliance Structure

- Establishing Controls & Standard
- Delegation of Responsibility
- Analysis & Assessment
- Compliance Reporting
- Updating of the amendments and latest modifications

Identification of General Laws need some more understanding. What are the laws to be applicable to the organization? This cannot be a sample list. It should be a comprehensive one. It also varies from Industry to Industry.

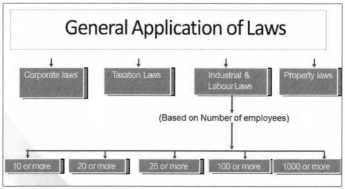

Figure 21 – Application of various laws

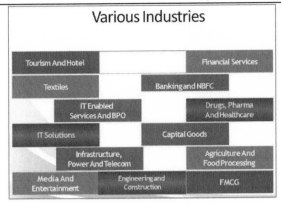

Figure 22 – Various Industries

Ok. What next? Developing a Compliance Management Tool –

Figure 23 – Checklist

NO END

No Complacence

Continue the Process...

Figure 24 – Continuous Process

Internal Controls

It has been mentioned as every organization should have a Policy, Procedure, Standard and Guidelines. Also, the organization should ensure that every employee be aware of all these. But importantly every organization should also ensure that every employee or even stakeholders strictly follow the policy and all. That is where a control comes into picture.

Hence Internal control, as defined by accounting and auditing, is a process for assuring of an organization's objectives in operational effectiveness and efficiency, reliable financial reporting and compliance with laws, regulations and policies.

Some examples of Internal Control in an accounting department - Internal control procedures document transactions by creating an audit trail. In the world of technology creating an audit trail is very easy and also, they are very much helpful in vigilance investigations. They limit the actions of employees by requiring authorization, approval and verification of selected transactions. They segregate duties because certain job responsibilities are mutually incompatible and if left unchecked, allow one person too much unsupervised access to company assets. No individual should be able to initiate a transaction and also approve it, record the information in accounting records and control the proceeds that result. This is what is called as "Maker-Checker" in IT parlance.

Internal controls are both preventive and detective. Preventive controls are designed to prevent errors, inaccuracy or fraud before it occurs. Detective controls are intended to uncover the existence of errors, inaccuracies or fraud that has already occurred.

Internal controls are one of the most essential elements within any organization. Internal controls are put in place to enable organizations to achieve their goals and missions. Management is responsible for the design, implementation and maintenance of all internal controls, with the Board responsible for the overall oversight of the control environment.

Strong internal controls allow the organizations to achieve three main objectives viz.,

- Accurate and reliable financial reporting
- Compliance with laws and regulations
- Effectiveness and efficiency of the organization's operations.

In order to achieve these objectives an internal control framework needs to be applied and followed throughout the organization. The five components of the internal control framework are;

- Control environment
- Risk assessment
- Control activities
- Information and communication
- Monitoring

Responsibilities and authority need to be assigned to different employees throughout an organization. Decision-making responsibilities should not be assigned to one individual alone. A proper internal control can be achieved using the below techniques;

- Segregate Accounting Duties
- Restrict Access to Financial Systems – role-based access
- Increase Oversight
- Have Financial Statements Reviewed by a Third Party

An effective internal control system includes organizational planning of a business and adopts all work-system and process to fulfill the targets like safeguarding business assets from stealing and wastage and ensuring compliance with business policies and the law of the land.

At it is most fundamental, a FI Corporate Compliance program is about ethics and managing conflicts of interest. Put simply, it is about doing the right thing.

Figure 25 – Compliance Framework

A Compliance Risk Framework is a tool that identifies, measures, documents and assesses compliance risk associated with a FI's activities, including:

- Development of new products/ services
- New business practices
- New types of business/ customer relationships
- Material changes to any of the above

Chapter Summary

Compliance has to be organization-wide and not a particular department or officer. There should be one specific officer called Compliance Officer, who can co-ordinate on the policies, procedures, standards and guidelines for the organization. However, it is not he and/or his department alone to be compliant. It is for the whole organization to be compliant.

Policies - Policies can be organization-wide, issue-specific or system specific. Organization's policies should reflect the objectives for information security program. Policies should be like a foundation of building - built to last and resistant to change or erosion. They are driven by business objectives and convey the amount of risk senior management is willing to accept.

Procedures - Procedures are detailed step by step instructions to achieve a given goal or mandate. They are typically intended for internal departments and should adhere to strict change control processes. Procedures can be developed as you go. If this is the route your organization chooses to take it's necessary to have comprehensive and consistent documentation of the procedures that you are developing.

Standards - Standards are mandatory actions or rules that give formal policies support and direction.

Guidelines - Guidelines are recommendations to users when specific standards do not apply. Guidelines are designed to streamline certain processes according to what the best practices are. Guidelines, by nature, should open to interpretation and do not need to be followed to the letter. They are more general vs. specific rules and provide flexibility for unforeseen circumstances.

Internal controls are processes put into place by management to help an organization operate efficiently and effectively to achieve its objectives. The fact is that management at all levels of an organization is responsible for ensuring that internal controls are set up, followed and reviewed periodically.

*****

Governance

Before understanding what is Governance, let us try to understand the words 'Administration' and 'Management'.

Management is all about plans and actions, but the administration is concerned with framing policies and setting objectives. The manager looks after the management of the organization, whereas administrator is responsible for the administration of the organization. Management focuses on managing people and their work. Management is an activity of business and functional level, whereas Administration is a high-level activity. While management focuses on policy implementation, policy formulation is performed by the administration.

Conceptually, governance (as opposed to 'good' governance) can be defined as the rule of the rulers, typically within a given set of rules. One might conclude that governance is the process – by which authority is conferred on rulers, by which they make the rules and by which those rules are enforced and modified. Thus, understanding governance requires an identification of the rulers and the rules, as well as the various processes by which they are selected, defined and linked together and with the society generally.

Origin of the word governance is from the Greek verb kubernáo which means to steer. As a process, governance operate in an organization of any size – from a single human being to all of humanity; and it may function for any purpose, good or evil, for profit or not. A reasonable or rational purpose of governance might aim to assure that an organization produces a worthwhile pattern of good results while avoiding an undesirable pattern of bad circumstances.

Good Governance - Within this concept of governance, the obvious second question is: What is good governance? Again, the debate on the quality of governance has been clouded by a slew of slightly differing definitions and understanding of what is actually meant by the term. Typically, it is defined in terms of the mechanisms thought to be needed to promote it. For example, in various places, good governance has been associated with transparency, with the rule of law and with efficient public services. For the cheque clearing process in banking scenario it would be finding a way to improve the efficiency of the person and there by process. How fast a cheque can be processed? Setting turnaround times, deadlines and consequence of meeting those should be explained to people involved in it. Making the person accountable for the delay.

Thus, the definition of good governance goes further than mechanisms and proposes that good governance be equated with specific outcomes. For example, the UNDP notes that: "Good governance is, among other things, participatory, transparent and accountable. It is also effective and equitable. And it promotes the rule of law. In general, the five dimensions of good governance that was developed in the World Bank's Corruption study for Europe and Central Asia is around public sector on this front:

✓ Public sector management,
✓ Competitive private sector,
✓ Structure of government,

✓ Civil society participation
✓ Political accountability.

This definition goes well beyond effective delivery of public and it can also go well beyond the notion of "economic governance" which is typically the focus of most World Bank work on governance.

Mechanisms for providing good governance have three key elements;

✓ *Internal rules and restraints* (for example, internal accounting and auditing systems, independence of the judiciary and the central bank, civil service and budgeting rules)
✓ *'Voice' and partnership* (for example, public-private deliberation councils and service delivery surveys to solicit client feedback)
✓ *Competition* (for example, competitive social service delivery, private participation in infrastructure, alternative dispute resolution mechanisms and outright privatization of certain market-driven activities).

Now, Governance is neither Administration nor Management. Governance is consistent management, cohesive policies, guidance, processes and decision-rights for a given area of responsibility and proper oversight and accountability.

> *Governance is neither Administration nor Management.*

In the context of GRC, in simple terms, managing risks and compliance is called Governance. In other words, risk management and governance management put together is governance.

Governance is managing risk and complying with various laws and whatever. This is the first part of **G**RC.

'GRC is the integrated collection of capabilities that enable an organization to reliably achieve objectives while addressing uncertainty and acting with integrity - this is the outcome that we call Principled Performance '[1]

— DCEG

'Every organizational business function and process is governed in some way to meet objectives. Each of these objectives has risks as well as controls that increase the likelihood of success (or minimize the impact of failure). These are the fundamental concepts of GRC.

— Forrester

Figure 26 – GRC Defined

Having had an overview of Risks and compliance, we need to manage both of them – that is really Governance.

The first scholarly research on GRC was published in 2007 and defined as "the integrated collection of capabilities that enable an organization to reliably achieve objectives, address uncertainty and act with integrity". Single goal of GRC is to "Keep the company on track".

Governance is the overall management approach through which senior executives direct and control the entire organization – a combination of management information and hierarchical management control structures.

Governance also ensures that critical management information reaching the executive team is sufficiently complete, accurate and timely to enable appropriate management decision making.

Governance provides the control mechanisms to ensure that strategies, directions and instructions from management are carried out systematically and effectively.

Governance is a system by which the organization is directed and controlled.

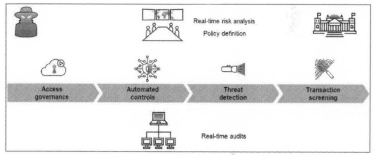

Figure 27 – Lower Risk & Higher Compliance

Types of governance

As described governance can exist in complex institutions, mechanisms, relationships and processes either formally or informally between or among the states, markets, citizens and organizations.

1. Regulatory Governance – Regulatory governance reflects the policy that needs to framed and followed by the system. It encourages the decentered and mutually adaptive policy regimes which rest on regulation. The term "Regulatory governance" deals with policy regimes which handle with complex system with a set of rules. It appears in arenas and nations which are more complex, global,

contested and democratic. Regulatory policy is instrument for governance.

2. Corporate Governance – Corporate governance is a set of processes, customs, policies, laws and institutions affecting the way people administer or control a corporation. Corporate governance includes many players and the corporate goals and the relationships among them. The principal players include the stakeholders, shareholders, management and the board of directors. Where the stakeholders include employees, suppliers, customers, banks and other lenders, regulators, the environment and the community at large.

Corporate governance involves a set of relationships between a company's Management, Board, Shareholders and Other stakeholders.

Corporate governance also provides the structure through which the objectives of the company are set and the means of attaining those objectives and monitoring performance are determined.

3. Project Governance – Information technology industry uses this term to the core and it describes the processes that need to exist for a successful project.

4. IT Governance – IT governance is primarily for connections between business focus and IT management. The goal of IT governance is to assure generation of business value for the investment made in IT and mitigate the risks that are associated with these IT projects.

5. Participatory Governance – Participatory governance focuses on involving citizen democratically in the processes of governance with the state. The idea behind such governance is citizens should play more direct roles in public decision-making or at least engage more deeply with political issues. Government officials should also be responsive to this kind of engagement. Best example is citizens casting their vote in elections i.e. the power of voting as voters is a form of participatory governance.

6. Non-profit Governance – Non-profit governance focuses primarily on the fiduciary responsibility that a board of trustees (sometimes called directors—the terms are interchangeable) has with respect to the exercise of authority over the explicit public trust that is understood to exist between the mission of an organization and those whom the organization serves.

7. Orders of Governance – Governance is becoming an increasingly complex issue with involvement of a variety of private as well as public actors

7.1 First Order Governance – This is the level at which problems are identified and solutions enacted. This is done through interaction between the governing organization and its citizens. It helps identifying;

✓ What is the problem?
✓ Who is experiencing it?
✓ What will be the best possible appropriate solution?

7.2 Second Order Governance – In this level the "institutional arrangements" are provided in many forms like the public or private sectors or combination of both. A framework is provided that enables first-order governance to take place.

Traditionally, Governance, Risk Management and Compliance have been seen as three separate and distinct disciplines, frameworks or processes within organizations. These three disciplines essentially serve to "keep the business on the rails as it travels to its destination".

They ensure that the organization moves towards achieving its objectives in a manner that is well structured and guided, mitigates risks and meets obligations to and expectations of stakeholders. A GRC program can be instituted to focus on any individual area(s) within the FI, or a fully integrated GRC, which will be able to work across all areas of the enterprise, using a single framework.

A fully integrated GRC uses a single core set of control materials, mapped to all of the primary governance factors being monitored. The use of a single framework also has the benefit of reducing the possibility of duplicated remedial actions.

> *Individual areas of GRC*
> - *Financial GRC*
>   - *IT GRC*
> - *Legal GRC*

When reviewed as individual GRC areas, the three most common individual headings are considered to be Financial GRC, IT GRC and Legal GRC.

- **Financial GRC** relates to the activities that are intended to ensure the correct operation of all financial processes, as well as compliance with any finance-related mandates.

- **IT GRC** relates to the activities intended to ensure that the IT (Information Technology) supports the current and future needs of the business and complies with all IT-related mandates.
- **Legal GRC** focuses on tying together all three components via an organization's legal department and chief compliance officer.

Analysts disagree on how these aspects of GRC are defined as market categories. It has stated that the broad GRC market includes the following areas;

1. Finance and audit GRC
2. IT GRC management
3. Enterprise risk management.

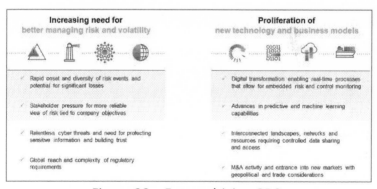

Figure 28 – Forces driving GRC

Integrated Risk Management within GRC

Governance, risk management and compliance are three related facets that help assure an organization reliably achieves objectives, addresses uncertainty and acts with integrity.

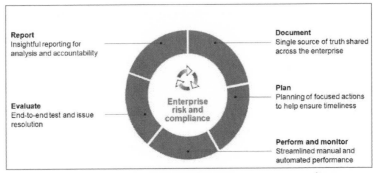

Figure 29 – Effective Control & On-going Compliance

IT Risk management being part of GRC, Information Security (IS) and GRC are attacked together.

GRC is a discipline that aims to synchronize information and activity across governance, risk management and compliance in order to operate more efficiently, enable effective information sharing, more effectively report activities and avoid wasteful overlaps.

The IT GRC management market is further divided into these key capabilities. Although this list relates to IT GRC, a similar list of capabilities would be suitable for other areas of GRC also.

> **Broad GRC Markets**
> - Finance and audit GRC
> - IT GRC management
> - Enterprise risk management.

- Controls and policy library
- Policy distribution and response
- IT Controls self-assessment and measurement
- IT Asset repository

- Automated general computer control (GCC) collection
- Remediation and exception management
- Reporting
- Advanced IT risk evaluation and compliance dashboards

Measuring Governance

Next question in line is "How to measure governance?" Measuring governance is a difficult task but several efforts are underway to measure the governance. These efforts have been conducted in the research and international development community and are in order to assess and measure the quality of governance of countries all around the world.

Measuring governance is inherently a controversial and political exercise. A distinction is therefore made between external assessments, peer assessments and self-assessments. Examples of external assessments are donor assessments or comparative indices produced by international non-governmental organizations.

Efforts are on to create an internationally comparable measure of governance by the members of the World Bank and the World Bank Institute. Members have identified the indicators for the following dimensions of governance:

- ➢ Voice and accountability,
- ➢ Political stability and lack of violence,
- ➢ Government effectiveness,
- ➢ Regulatory quality,
- ➢ Rule of law,

➤ Control of corruption.

A new World Governance Index (WGI) has been developed and is open for improvement through public participation.

Point solutions to governance, risk and compliance are marked by their focus on addressing only one of these areas (governance or risk or compliance). In some cases of limited requirements, these solutions can serve a viable purpose. However, because they tend to have been designed to solve domain specific problems in great depth, they generally do not take a unified approach and are not tolerant of integrated governance requirements. Information systems will address these matters better if the requirements for governance, risk and compliance management are incorporated at the design stage, as part of a coherent framework.

GRC data warehousing and business intelligence

GRC vendors with an integrated data framework are now able to offer custom built GRC data warehouse and business intelligence solutions. This allows high value data from any number of existing governances, risk and compliance applications to be collated and analyzed.

The aggregation of GRC data using this approach adds significant benefit in the early identification of risk and business process (and business control) improvement.

Further benefits to this approach include;

(i) It allows existing, specialist and high value applications to continue without impact

(ii) Organizations can manage an easier transition into an integrated GRC approach because the initial change is only adding to the reporting layer and

(iii) It provides a real-time ability to compare and contrast data value across systems that previously had no common data scheme.

Integrated GRC in FIs – A recent survey on the "Changing FI's Landscape" to jointly get a better understanding of how the FIs services' market will develop. Here are a few of the major conclusions.

1. FIs are strapped by new regulations, which risks to make it very hard for them to deliver the services the corporate sector needs.

2. FIs are deleveraging and withdrawing from different areas opening up for new entrants. The question is: who will be those new entrants?

3. Will there be global FIs, or even FIs aspiring to be global and how does that affect product areas such as cross border trade?

4. Technology and new solutions will push FIs out from parts of the financial supply chain

5. FI products risk to be more expensive

6. Corporates need to be more alert of changing counterparties and have lots of more relations active

The emergence of GRC based – Enterprise Risk Management (ERM).

We live in a perilous world, as we speak the US Federal Reserve prepares to embrace for the current economic environment without using the 'R' word and that R word is not 'risks' or proactive "risk management". It is reactive 'Recession'. From meltdowns in the mortgage industry, terrible weather and natural disasters in your global operations, lead paint in toys to corporate executives detailing your company's financial performance on social blogosphere – threats are everywhere. And so are opportunities, diverse, interconnected and complex such as disruptive innovation, new regulatory mandates and competitor missteps. As put by a Chief Risk Officer of a global financial institution, "Risks create opportunity; opportunity in turn creates value; and that value ultimately creates shareholder wealth"

Almost half of the 1000 large global companies suffered declines in share prices of more than 20 percent in a one-month period, relative to the Morgan Stanley Capital International (MSCI) World Index. By the end of first decade of this century, roughly one-quarter of these companies had still not recovered their lost market value. Another one-quarter took more than a year for their share prices to recover. With the emergence of unified Governance, Risk and Compliance (GRC) based ERM solution – firms are no longer surrounded by reactive measures that cause shareholder value to decline and cause a decline in corporate goodwill and responsibility in the marketplace. An effective GRC program covers all tenants of effective strategic management – ethical corporate governance, where the CEO sets the tone for the business strategy and the Board is empowered by real-time visibility into operational details i.e. the realities – of this vision's material weakness. GRC covers risks that emanate from multi-regulatory and compliance management initiatives, that include dealing with SOX, SEC, PCAOB, ISO, FCPA, FDA, cGxP, FERC, NERC, COBIT, PRIVACY, IP, BASEL, AML, GREEN TECH, EH&S, 21 CFR, FAA and so on. In the past, large or small firms each mandate had its own program, its own team and its own tool and hence businesses were playing catch-up.

GRC intermediates the prevalence of this silo approach by combining these silos into a single program that simply enables the firm to be proactive in its approach to dealing with these myriads of complexities. However, GRC can be effective only if the right priorities are visible at the right time to the right stakeholder.

ERM is hence the central convent of a unified approach to GRC. ERM is the means to prioritize and manage risks and opportunities across a firm in a way that it generates greater business value. ERM pays for itself by reducing financial losses, improving business performance and enhancing risk identification and assessment efforts.

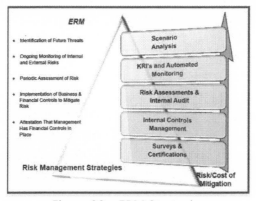

Figure 30 – ERM Strategies

Sample Risk Types

In 2005, Hurricane Katrina cost insurers more than $41 billion, the largest loss event ever for the industry. The magnitude of losses eventually reported shocked many. In the wake of the disaster, ERM was a differentiating element when we reviewed insurer credit ratings. Some insurers with weaker ERM had losses that were as much as twice what they previously reported as their "probable maximum loss". These insurers were unable to even estimate their losses several days after the event. On the other hand, insurers with stronger ERM could quickly estimate losses that were within 25% of actual claims.

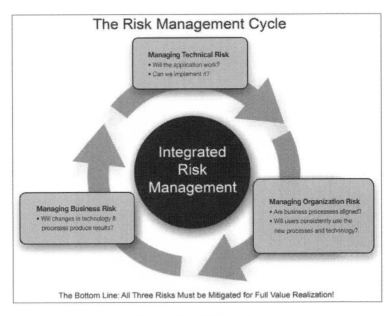

Figure 31 – ERM Cycle

New guidance to identify risks affecting shareholder value

"The ERM Evaluation ultimately will be our opinion of the quality of management practices" – a credit bureau

Our interest in codifying management analysis under the ERM heading coincides with increased interest by many companies to initiate their own ERM programs –- or other risk-management practices – to increase risk-adjusted returns, improve strategic judgment and/ or avoid extraordinary losses due to lawsuits, fines, operational failures, or negligence. The intersection of these interests is in the expectation that a firm's future ability to meet financial obligations in full and on time is more likely to be enhanced by strong ERM or diminished by weak or nonexistent ERM. Our principal interest in evaluating ERM is to implement steps that will limit the frequency and severity of losses that could potentially affect ratings.

This new guidance is primarily aimed at helping financial and non-financial services customers to have a management that values ERM to and has a clear strategy to mitigate losses in shareholder value. They have introduced Enterprise Risk Management (ERM) analysis into the corporate credit ratings processes to provide guidance via means of a structured framework to evaluate the company's management as a principal component in determining the overall business profile – they intend to take Enterprise Risk Management (ERM) into their analysis of business and its impact on corporate credit ratings. This undertaking and will impact a wide range of verticals namely - Manufacturing, Commodities, Utilities, Consumer, Healthcare, Technology, Media, Telecommunications and so on. The wide-reaching impact will see other rating agencies use basic ERM frameworks in their analysis of businesses.

With superior ERM ratings to have less volatility in earnings and cash flow and will optimize the risk/ return relationship. Furthermore, they intend to use these ratings to serve as industry wide risk management benchmarking.

An analysis deems financial services firms, due to the nature of their business, intrinsically riskier than non-financial services organizations; and hence in contrast the ratings process for the non-financial services organizations would be a verdict of the efficacy of the management to execute the vision of the company and build shareholder value.

Environment Risks	Financial Risks	Supply Risks	Management Risks
Business Continuity	Capital availability	Commodity Prices	Corporate Governance
Business Market Environment	Credit/ Counterparty	Supply Chain	Data Security
Environmental	Financial Market Risk		Employee health and Safety
Liability lawsuits	Inflation		Intellectual Property
Natural Disasters/ Weather	Interest Rates		Labor Disputes
Pandemic	Liquidity		Labor Skills shortage
Physical damage			M&A/ Restructuring

Political risk			Managing complexity
Regulatory/ Legislative			Outsourcing problems

The scoring methodology will have companies scored in four primary categories: weak, adequate, strong and excellent – the scoring weight would factor in the relative significance of ERM in the vertical industry. Where companies rated 'weak' display low levels of ERM maturity – complete absence of controls, in contrast with those rated 'excellent' are mature companies with a comprehensive program of leadership, process, people and technology to manage risks.

A Conference Board report which studied US and European attitudes towards ERM found that the companies that have already implemented ERM reported a 'significantly' higher level of value added than those without ERM programs. The biggest pluses were better informed decisions (86 per cent with ERM, 58 per cent for others), greater management consensus (83 per cent with ERM, 36 per cent for others) and increased accountability (79 per cent with ERM, 34 per cent without). A better understanding of operational and strategic risks was also seen as a key benefit. Additional benefits reported were better strategic planning and a greater ability to understand the risk/reward equation in decision making. The study also revealed that the trend towards ERM is helping risk management gain greater acceptance throughout organizations. The highest priority objectives for survey respondents were ensuring risks are considered in decision-making and avoiding surprises and predictable failures.

Four major analytic components or 'pillars will support the ERM analysis; these factors are broad, sector agnostic views into the risks faced by the firm. These include:

- Analysis of making routine corporate decisions
- Analysis of risk controls
- Analysis of emerging risk preparation
- Analysis of strategic risk management

Enterprise Risk Management Framework

Risk management culture and governance provides visibility of importance of "risk taking" or lack of in routine decision making – within the company's corporate culture. A firm's maturity would be evaluated by assessing its structure, roles and responsibilities to execute ERM. The visibility that the top-management has to daily execution issues with line management and the rendezvous that occurs to communicate and collaborate on routine decision making are firm indicators of a winning ERM strategy.

Risk controls help organizations implement the culture and governance, through identifying, measuring and on-going monitoring, reconciling risk, setting risk limits and arrive at the firm's daily profile for managing risks in a distributed world. The market intends to develop an exhaustive list of controls across sector and firm – and depending upon the relative weight of each control will help painting a picture of the firm's overall ERM efforts.

Incorporate the ideas of risk, risk management and return for risk into corporate strategic decision-making and planning processes.

Emerging risk preparation – the black swan effect author Nassim Nicholas Tasseb in a recent book ventures out to talk about the black swan affect that can have on a firm's long-term survival. These are the types of risks that are extremely rare adverse events and are impossible to manage in a control environment. However, some ERM best practices – can help a firm remain prepared for addressing such scenarios coming to life. Preparedness includes environmental scanning, trend analysis, stress testing, contingency planning, problem post-mortem and risk transfer. A firm's ability to prepare itself for the best or the worst of will also need to be factored into the Risk profile.

Strategic Risk Management will help to arrive at a single classification of the firms ERM standing or profile – this could be expressed in terms of earnings loss, Risk profile can be expressed in terms of earnings loss, enterprise value, or other important financial metrics for various risks or for each firm business.

The essence of planning for the future as a progressive firm is changing. Infinite – risk/ reward possibilities, disparate and complex threats are in the face of today's vibrant and interconnected global firm. Old adages on risk – and reward are still worth their value in gold, however they now require several additional people, process, organization and technology "upgrades" for firms to survive and thrive. ERM hence will provide the leaders of the organization – a means to increase earnings – and shareholder value – whilst staying within the well-defined and organizationally absorbed risk tolerance.

Chapter Summary

Governance is neither Administration nor Management.

In the context of GRC, in simple terms, managing risks and compliance is called Governance. In other words, risk management and governance management put together is governance.
Governance is managing risk and complying with various laws and whatever. This is the first part of **G**RC.

Single goal of GRC is to "Keep the company on track".

The governance process vary organization to organization, business to business, industry to industry. Hence "one size does not fit all".

A firm's ability to prepare itself for the best or the worst of will also need to be factored into the Risk profile.

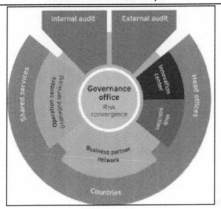

*****

Governance Vs e-Governance

When any activity is done using electronic media then 'e' is prefixed to it. For instance, banking – e-banking, payment – e-payment, filing – e-filing, etc. Similarly, when a governance is done electronically then it is e-Governance.

The generic e-Governance or e-GRC framework is depicted in this diagram.

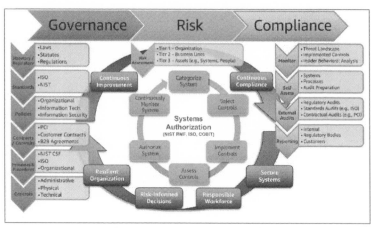

Figure 32 – GRC Framework

Electronic governance - e-Governance can be understood as is the utilization of information and communication technology (ICT) for providing services, disseminating information, communication activities and incorporation of miscellaneous standalone systems and services between different models, processes and interaction within the overall structure.

e-Governance is the application of IT to the process of Governing body functioning to bring about;

- <u>S</u>mart
- <u>M</u>oral
- <u>A</u>ccountable
- <u>R</u>esponsive
- <u>T</u>ransparent Governance

e-Governance is a tool, that makes available various services in a convenient way, such as;

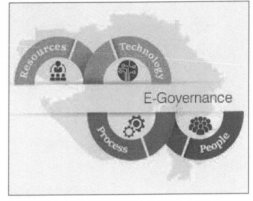

- Better provision of services
- Improved interaction with different groups
- Stakeholder/ Client/ Customer empowerment through access to information
- Efficient/ effective management

It is about using technology for process and people with

the available resources. It always depends in Industry, business and particular organization.

e-Government is a system whereas e-Governance is a functionality. Government means the application of ICT in government operations, as a tool to make better government. e-Governance, on the other hand, implies the use of ICT in transforming and supporting functions and structures of the system e-Governance is the integration of Information and Communication Technology (ICT) in all the processes, with the aim of enhancing the ability to address the needs of the stakeholders. In short, it is the use of electronic means, to promote good governance.

The Advantages of e-Governance can be;

- Improves delivery and efficiency of services.
- Improved interactions with business and industry.
- Stakeholder empowerment through access to information.
- More efficient management.
- Less corruption in the administration.
- Increased transparency in administration – The average organization today is a complex organism with multiple people, hierarchies, business lines, suppliers/ vendors and global operations. The greater the complexity, the more difficult is it to ensure risk transparency. But the more the risk transparency, the more value the organization holds in the eyes of investors. Greater risk transparency also allows management to make smarter and more informed strategic decisions.

The two main objectives of e-Governance are to meet the goal to its true meaning with the help of improvisation of the participation of the stakeholders in the governing process by giving feedback and access to information and overall participation of the relevant resources in the decision making.

The e-Governance can be implemented in stages like;

- Web presence – this phase is the most basic form of e-government.
- Interaction,
- Transaction,
- Transformation
- e-Democracy.

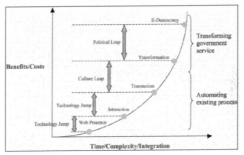

Figure 33 – e-Governance Time-benefit comparison

Some extract of a live research paper about e-Governance in a bank, is appended below for easy understanding. The author of this book was the guide for this research. Thought the research was specific to Indian environment and a little bit old in age, the concepts are still worthy.

Traditionally, the interaction between customer and business or a private agency or government agency took place in the latter's office. With emerging information and communication technologies like internet, kiosk, mobile banking etc., it is possible to bring these parties more closely. These kinds of advancements have forced the respective agencies to manage their day to day activities more innovatively to satisfy the customer keeping in mind the regulatory compliance. Agencies have to re-establish the set of policies, roles, responsibilities and processes to guide, direct the organization. Also, to control how the organization uses technologies to accomplish business goals and thereby satisfy the customer. This has paved way to a new way of handling the requests and related compliance called e-governance.

Such improvements can serve a variety of different ends;

✓ Better delivery of services to customers,
✓ Improved interactions with business and industry,
✓ Customer empowerment through access to information, or
✓ More efficient management.

The resulting benefits can result in less time, increased transparency, greater convenience, revenue growth and/ or cost reductions.

E-Governance in Banks – MMP

The Banking MMP is yet another step towards improving operational efficiency and reducing the delays and efforts involved in handling and settling transactions. The MMP which is being implemented by the banking industry aims at streamlining various e-services initiatives undertaken by individual banks. Implementation is being done by the banks concerned, with the banking Department providing a broad framework and guidance.

Technology has completely transformed basic paradigms in banking. Technology has allowed banks to reduce costs, increase customer service and increase by multiple-folds transaction volumes.

Banks today are one of the greatest adopters of technology and while there is a growing awareness and movement towards adopting technology, banks often are blind to the vulnerabilities these technologies bring.

Networking and telecommunications are one of main reason for banking revolution. Apart from this software revolution too is one of the major factors. Evolution of core banking technology in India has brought in the convenience of "anytime, anywhere banking" to Indian customers. Core banking system is a system that processes daily banking transactions and posts updates to accounts and other financial records. Core banking systems include deposit, loan and credit-processing capabilities. It also interfaces to general ledger systems and reporting tools.

There is now a movement towards integration of core banking solutions of various banks, which is expected to bring in operational efficiency and reduce the time and effort involved in handling and settling transactions, thereby improving customer service and facilitating regulatory compliance.

Governance in banks traditionally has been manual resulting in more time. This was mainly due to time consuming processes and compliance. Adding on, there were also location constraints.

e-Governance – in and through Banks – Banking Mission Mode Programs (MMP) provides vision and objective for achieving operational efficiency. Three major factor which help in achieving operational efficiency and quality services are

➢ Internet, Networking Communication
➢ Software Capability
➢ Hardware infrastructural facilities and capability to support the above factors.

Apart from banking industry organization there are different wings of the government which utilizes the banking services. These organizations are also benefitted out of the banking MMP outcomes.

A bank should first make itself technologically advanced and thus achieve the ultimate goal of e-governance by offering it's the services to the common man or public domain in such a way that it is easily accessible. While attaining this objective of the banking MMP bank is also used as means to provide the e-governance services of the other departments.

Thus, a bank can be a;

➢ e-Governance in Banks - Initiator – Where bank itself has implemented its Banking MMP
➢ e-Governance Enabler – Where a bank offers the e-governance initiatives of the several other government departments through its channels.

The advancement in technology, especially Internet and information technology has led to new ways of doing business in banking. This technology has cut down time, working simultaneously on different issues and there-by increasing efficiency. The platform where communication technology and information technology are merged to suit core needs of banking is called as core banking solutions and many banks have implemented this Core Banking solution.

Core banking means services provided by a bank by networking its bank branches. CORE stands for "Centralized Online Real-time Environment". Bank customers can access their funds and other simple transactions from any of the branch offices spread across the globe. Thus, ensuring the "One India One account" objective.

In core banking the bank's branches access applications from a centralized data center. Any deposits made are reflected immediately on the bank's servers and the customer can withdraw the deposited money from any of the bank's branches throughout the globe. Needs of corporate customers are also addressed by these applications by providing a comprehensive banking solution.

Normal core banking functions will include deposit accounts, loans, mortgages and payments. Banks make these services available to the mass across multiple channels like ATMs, Internet banking and branches.

Computer software is developed to perform banks core operations of like recording of transactions in journal and ledger, passbook maintenance, interest calculations on loans and deposits, customer records, balance of payments and withdrawal. It also has interface to many systems including reporting tool.

This software is installed at different branches of bank and then interconnected by means of communication lines like telephones, satellite, internet etc. It allows the user (customers) to operate accounts from any branch if it has installed core banking solutions. This new platform has changed the way banks are working.

Strategic spending on these systems is based on a combination of service-oriented architecture and supporting technologies that create extensible, agile architectures

Chapter Summary;

When a governance is done electronically then it is e-Governance. It should fit into a framework.

e-Governance can be understood as is the utilization of information and communication technology (ICT) for providing services, disseminating information, communication activities and incorporation of miscellaneous stand-alone systems and services between different models, processes and interaction within the overall structure.

The two main objectives of e-Governance are to meet the goal to its true meaning with the help of improvisation of the participation of the stakeholders in the governing process by giving feedback and access to information and overall participation of the relevant resources in the decision making.

The e-Governance cannot be implemented in one-go, but has to be in stages.

GRC Technology

GRC technology enables agile and resilient risk management processes by providing a common platform to collaborate, exchange information and conduct reporting. It also helps the organizations to eliminate manual activities and create greater efficiency within each line of defense.

Managing risk, compliance and governance with GRC technology removes redundant processes and tasks, which results in reduced costs. The latest GRC solution also incorporate automation and artificial intelligence (AI) into the system which speeds up and automates processes. This is important because it allows organizations to demonstrate resilience, allocate resources, make appropriate decisions to reduce risk whilst managing compliance with regulations/ frameworks.

GRC Technology Services assist clients with identifying technology requirements to support their GRC processes, selecting GRC vendors, implementing technology platforms and performing a post deployment review to assess lessons learned from the implementation.

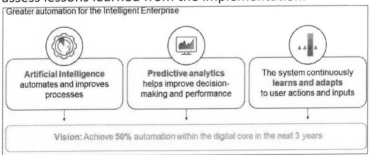

Figure 34 – Digitization of GRC

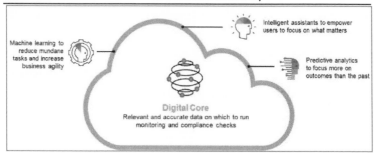

Figure 35 – New Technologies in GRC

GRC Products[2]

The distinctions between the sub-segments of the broad GRC market are often not clear. With a large number of vendors entering this market recently, determining the best product for a given business problem can be challenging. Given that the analysts do not fully agree on the market segmentation, vendor positioning can increase the confusion. The governance process vary organization to organization, business to business, industry to industry. Hence "one size does not fit all".

Due to the dynamic nature of this market, any vendor analysis is often out of date relatively soon after its publication.

Broadly, the vendor market can be considered to exist in 3 segments;

• Integrated governance, risk and compliance solutions (multi-governance interest, enterprise wide)

---

[2] Both this book and the author are product/ vendor agnostic. Just to have an understanding of the market by the beginners with the nuances these are being discussed here.

- Domain specific GRC solutions (single governance interest, enterprise wide)
- Point solutions to governance, risk or compliance (relate to enterprise wide governance or enterprise wide risk or enterprise wide compliance but not in combination).

Integrated governance, risk and compliance solutions attempt to unify the management of these areas, rather than treat them as separate entities. An integrated solution is able to administer one central library of compliance controls, but manage, monitor and present them against every governance factor. For example, in a domain specific approach, three or more findings could be generated against a single broken activity. The integrated solution recognizes this as one break relating to the mapped governance factors.

Domain specific governance, risk and compliance vendors understand the cyclical connection between governance, risk and compliance within a particular area of governance. For example, within financial processing — that a risk will either relate to the absence of a control (need to update governance) and/ or the lack of adherence to (or poor quality of) an existing control.

An initial goal of splitting out GRC into a separate market has left some vendors confused about the lack of movement. It is thought that a lack of deep education within a domain on the audit side, coupled with a mistrust of audit in general causes a rift in a corporate environment. However, there are vendors in the marketplace that, while remaining domain-specific, have begun marketing their product to end users and departments that, while either tangential or overlapping, have expanded to include the internal corporate internal audit (CIA) and external audit teams. This approach provides a more "open book" approach into the process. If the production team will be audited by CIA using an application that production also has access to, is thought to reduce risk more quickly as the end goal is not to be 'compliant' but to be 'secure,' or as secure as possible.

Top GRC tools are;

- Content management.
- Document management.
- User event input/ output, distribution and communication.
- Risk analytics.
- Risk and control management.
- Workflow management.
- Audit management.
- Dashboards and reporting.

As a suggestion or analysis here are some of the most used governance risk and compliance software solutions – repeat just for analysis and comparison only;

- IBM OpenPages.
- ServiceNow Governance Risk and Compliance.
- SAI Global Compliance 360.
- Navex Global Risk Rate.
- Enablon.
- Riskonnect.
- SAP GRC.
- Nasdaq BWise.

The GRC Market

Some expert predictions on the trends and developments to look out for in 2020, analyze the GRC market in extraordinary depth. Market segmentation, trends, drivers, growth, forecasting and more were studied in detail. It also drilled down into technological innovations liable to impact the market in the months and years ahead.

One major takeaway from the is "change is the greatest challenge impacting GRC management".

The regulatory, legal, business and risk environments are evolving every day and can all impact an organization and complicate the task of GRC professionals.

Another factor is the movement towards expecting accountability versus responsibility from executives and company leaders.

The impact of the Senior Managers Regime is another topic that is insights on the regulation.

The need to meet all these challenges is why enterprises are turning to GRC technologies as never before.

The GRC market is being flooded with providers. Much as the legal technology sector has seen a huge influx of investment as scores of startups appear almost weekly, the GRC market has seen a flood of would-be technology and service providers. The study points out how there are 843 technology vendors that offer GRC-related solutions and over 1,000 professional services firms have cropped up with GRC offerings.

That should not surprise anyone, since the opportunities are expanding so remarkably. The Risk Management technology segment alone saw over $2.5 billion in sales in 2019. The enterprise GRC tech market was the runner-up, at over $1.6 billion. The total GRC tech market is over $8.9 billion.

Chapter Summary;

GRC technology enables agile and resilient risk management processes. Managing risk, compliance and governance with GRC technology removes redundant processes and tasks, which results in reduced costs.
There are various GRC tools and different vendors enter into the market with the help AI based solutions.

Still no single solution can help all the businesses, since the processes vary organization to organization.

The total GRC tech market is calculated to be over $8.9 billion and still increasing.

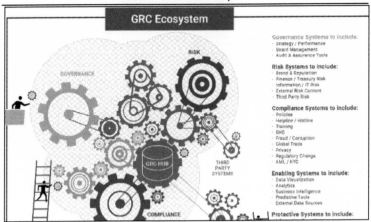

Figure 36 – GRC Eco-system

*****

GRC Audit

What is Audit? - Audit is the examination or inspection of various books of accounts by an auditor followed by physical checking of inventory to make sure that all departments are following documented system of recording transactions. It is done to ascertain the accuracy of financial statements provided by the organization.

What is GRC Audit? GRC audit on the other hand is to verify whether risk and compliance management related policies, procedures, etc., are all in place, they are updated & adequate and they are strictly followed by all the employees of the organizations. To verify - As a structured approach to aligning IT with business objectives, while effectively managing risk and meeting compliance requirements.

Systematic process of objectively obtaining and evaluating evidences regarding assertions and ascertain the degree of correspondence between the assertions and established policies and procedures and communicating the results to the stakeholders.

In general, an audit is an investigation of an existing system, report, or entity. There are a number of types of audits that can be conducted, including the following;

Compliance audit – An examination of the policies and procedures of an entity or department, to see if it is in compliance with internal or regulatory standards. This audit is most commonly used in regulated industries or educational institutions.

Construction audit – An analysis of the costs incurred for a specific construction project. Activities may include an analysis of the contracts granted to contractors, prices paid, overhead costs allowed for reimbursement, change orders and the timeliness of completion. The intent is to ensure that the costs incurred for a project were reasonable.

Financial audit – An analysis of the fairness of the information contained within an entity's financial statements. It is conducted by a CPA firm, which is independent of the entity under review. This is the most commonly conducted type of audit.

IS audit – A review of the controls over software development, data processing and access to computer systems. The intent is to spot any issues that could impair the ability of IT systems to provide accurate information to users, as well as to ensure that unauthorized parties do not have access to the data.

Investigative audit – An investigation of a specific area or individual when there is a suspicion of inappropriate or fraudulent activity. The intent is to locate and remedy control breaches, as well as to collect evidence in case charges are to be brought against someone.

Operational audit – A detailed analysis of the goals, planning processes, procedures and results of the operations of a business. The audit may be conducted internally or by an external entity. The intended result is an evaluation of operations, likely with recommendations for improvement.

Tax audit – An analysis of the tax returns submitted by an individual or business entity, to see if the tax information and any resulting income tax payment is valid. These audits are usually targeted at returns that result in excessively low tax payments, to see if an additional assessment can be made.

Cost audit – the verification of cost accounts and check on the adherence to cost accounting plan. It ascertains the accuracy of cost accounting records to ensure that they are in conformity with Cost Accounting principles, plans, procedures and objective.

Management audit – is an assessment of how well an organization's management team is applying its strategies and resources. A management audit evaluates whether the management team is working in the interests of shareholders, employees and the company's reputation.

SOX audit – A SOX compliance audit of a company's internal controls takes place once a year. An independent auditor must conduct SOX audits. It is the company's responsibility to find and hire an auditor and to arrange all necessary meetings prior to when the audit takes place.

IFRS audit – IFRS audit is to verify whether the accounting is as per the IFRS-IAS standards.

Internal audit – is a dynamic profession involved in helping organizations achieve their objectives. It is concerned with evaluating and improving the effectiveness of risk management, control and governance processes in an organization.

Concurrent audit – is a systematic and timely examination of transactions on a regular basis in parallel to ensure accuracy, authenticity, compliance with procedures and guidelines. The emphasis under concurrent audit is not on test checking but on substantial checking of transactions.

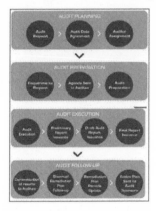

Figure 37 – Audit Life Cycle

Audit life-cycle

An audit cycle is the process that auditors employ in conducting any audit. The audit cycle includes the steps that an auditor will take to ensure that the information is valid and accurate before releasing any report. The audit cycle can call for different tasks to be performed at different times - for example, audit planning, audit preparation, audit execution and audit follow-up.

Typical audit cycle would have different phases of audit process like;

- Audit Planning
- Audit Kick Off

- Audit Process
  - Sub-processes
  - Audit control, etc.
- Audit Execution/ Control Test
- Audit Communication

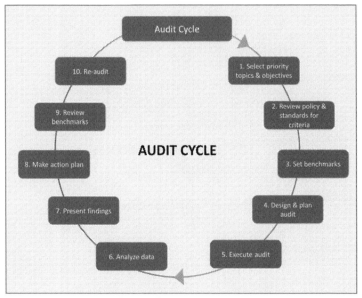

Figure 38 – Elaborated Audit Life Cycle

Audit Planning is the first phase of an audit life cycle. Audit communication is the last phase. These two are very vital phases also and at the same time, that much importance is not given by auditors. Lot many audits fail to meet the objective, because of wrong planning and/ or wrong communication. Hence these two phases are being elaborated in this book.

Audit Planning

This has various steps like;

- Requirements from sponsors request
- Accept the client and perform initial audit planning
- Understand the client's business and industry
- Assess client business risk
- Perform preliminary analytical procedures
- Set materiality and assess acceptable audit risk and inherent risk
- Understand internal control and assess control risk
- Pre-audit questionnaire request to the company to be audited
- Risk Evaluation performance
- Objectives and Audit Approach definition
- Agenda preparation and sending
- Audit records preparation
- Develop overall audit plan and program

Audit planning helps the auditor in a number of ways including;

- Giving suitable attention to important or high-risk areas of audit engagements.
- Identifying and resolving problems in a timely manner.
- Organizing and managing an audit effectively and efficiently.
- Selecting audit team members and in assigning work to them.
- Helps the auditor in directing, supervising audit engagements and also to carry out review of the work of team members.

Audit planning is not a standalone stage of an audit which takes place at the start of every audit.

Audit Planning is a continuous process. It usually starts at the conclusion of the previous audit and continues until current audit is concluded. However, planning involves the consideration of nature, timing and resources required to perform an engagement.

The auditor may wish to discuss the components of planning (at the pre-audit meeting) to make the engagement efficient. However, care should be taken not to discuss to the extent that it negatively affects the effectiveness of the audit by making It too predictable and thus giving management the chance to circumvent audit procedures.

At the commencement of current audit engagement before any other significant activities take place, auditor is required to perform the following procedures;

Perform procedures regarding client continuance and specific audit engagement.

- Evaluation of compliance with ethical requirement of the engagement team (Integrity & independence)
- Agreeing the terms of engagement with the client and understanding of such terms. Performing such initial activity enables the auditor to identify any problem right from the beginning of an engagement which may affect the audit adversely.

The audit planning activities inter-alia include the design of an audit strategy which sets out;

- Scope

- Timing & duration
- Direction of the audit engagement.
- Once audit strategy is in place, audit plan can then be developed on the basis of the audit strategy.

An audit strategy outlines the OBJECTIVES of the audit that is to be performed – like crafting the skeleton of a body. A strategy is like understanding the entity and its environment, E.g. ICS (Internal Control Systems) and risk and materiality?

In determining audit strategy, the auditor;

- Determines the characteristics of the engagement that defines the scope. E.g. applicable laws, users of audit report, number of branches to be visited, etc.
- Identify the reporting objective of the engagement
- Nature of the communication required. E.g. Deadline for interim report, stock taking schedule, etc.
- Consider other important factors that will determine the direction of the audit engagement.
- Determine the nature and extent of resources required to perform the audit

The good perspective of audit as "fault finding missions" have gone. At that time the auditors were looked at "un-invited visitors". But nowadays, auditors are all guides and audits are being looked at recommendations for improvement.

It is a known fact that the primary responsibility of an auditor is not to detect fraud. However, detection of fraud by an auditor is as a result of a well-planned audit.

Once audit strategy is in place, audit plan can then be developed which include the description of;

- The nature, timing and extent of risk assessment procedures control risk + Inherent risk + Detection risk = Total audit risk. Even a "risk management audit" is prone for risk. Auditors also have to undergo a risk called "Audit risk".
- The nature, timing and extent of further audit procedures (substantive tests or extended substantive tests)
- The nature, timing and extent of other audit procedures

Planning is not a onetime activity, auditor may need to revisit the audit strategy and audit plan as changes in situation dictates (changes in nature, timing, extent of audit procedure). Such changes can occur due to;

- Unexpected event
- Changes in condition e.g. scope
- Audit evidence – The auditor may become aware of discrepancies in accounting records, or conflicting or missing evidence.
- Acquiring information that is significantly different from the information the auditor had as at the time of planning.
- The extent of misstatements that the auditor detects while performing substantive procedures may alter the auditor's judgment about the risk assessments and may indicate a significant deficiency in internal control.

- Analytical procedures performed at the overall review stage of the audit may indicate a previously unrecognized risk of material misstatement

In such circumstances, the auditor may need to reevaluate the planned audit procedures, based on the revised consideration of assessed risks for all or some of the classes of transactions, account balances, or disclosures and related assertions.

Audit Kick-off

The following are the activating during the Audit kick-off stage;

- Finalizing the scope of audit
- Setting the expectation with the top executives
- Discussing with the auditees
- Finalizing the duration
- Finalizing the report submission mode – softcopy, hardcopy, etc.

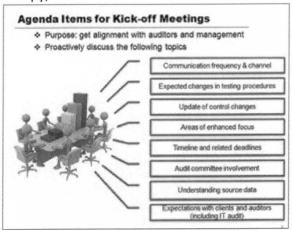

Figure 39 – Audit Kick-Off Meeting Agenda

Audit Execution

Once the audit is planned, fieldwork is executed by the Auditor(s). It can be in any mode like;

- Interviewing/ discussion with the auditees
- Discussing with the auditees
- Clients are kept informed of the audit process through regular status meetings.
- Audit observations, potential findings and recommendations are discussed with the client as they are identified.

Some of the specific steps in the audit process that should be followed to ensure a successful audit;

- Requesting necessary Documents
- Preparing an Audit Plan and communicating with the client
- Scheduling discussions with various teams
- Conducting Onsite Fieldwork

DURING THE AUDIT... The Audit Team will:

- Collect & record objective evidence
- Verify observations
- Record non-conformances
- Evaluate information and ensure validity

Figure 40 – Audit Execution

In an audit evidence gathering is the systematic process of gathering evidence about entity's operations, evaluating it and finding out those operations meet the acceptable standards. The evidences can be;

- Physical
- Documentary
- Testimonial
- Analytical.

Whatever be the format, the evidences should be sufficient, appropriate relevant, competent and useful.

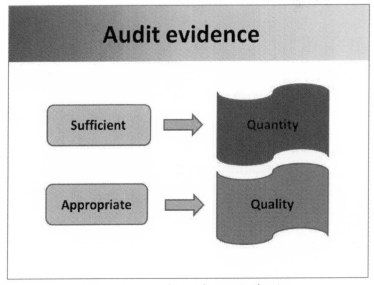

Figure 41 – Audit Evidence Gathering

It is for the auditor ascertain that the existing evidences are complete and accurate.

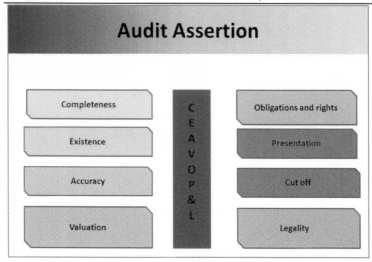

Figure 42 – Audit Assertion

Audit Communication

Good old standard focused on communication of audit matters arising from the audit was essentially a one-way communication from auditor to the client.

Now the latest standard imposes specific obligation on auditor to promote effective two-way communication. Auditor now has specific responsibility to take steps to achieve effective two-way communication, or failing that, to take further appropriate action. Emphasis on effective two-way communication should be recognized in the objectives of audit.

Two-way communication is important, because it;

- Assists in developing constructive working relationship between auditor and the client.

- Sets clear expectations between auditor and the client regarding communication of matters of audit relevance.
- Recognizes that the client is an important element of control environment.
- Assists the client in fulfilling their oversight responsibility for financial reporting process.
- Recognizes that the client is an important source of information for conduct of effective audit.

It is for the auditor to decide and evaluate whether two-way communication has been adequate. If two-way communication is not adequate, it may affect auditor's assessment of risks of material misstatement and may affect auditor's ability to obtain sufficient appropriate audit evidence. New auditing standards provide guidance on possible auditor actions.

Communication form, timing and expected general content of communications;

- Provides basis for constructive dialogue
- Helps to explain or clarify such matters as
- Purpose of communications
- Which person(s) on each side will be the point contacts
- The auditor's expectation that the communication will be two-way
- How the feedback mechanism will work between the parties

The communication process will not be the same as in a larger entity audit. The Process will vary with entity's size and governance structure, among other things. Formal communications may be more appropriate in a larger entity audit. Greater formality may be necessary with greater size and complexity of entity.

Less structured approach often more suitable in an SME audit, consistent with lack of formality in management and governance practices in SMEs. Often, oral communication may be all that is needed in an SME audit, especially if auditor has ongoing contact and dialogue with the client.

If all the clients are involved in managing the entity, matters communicated with them in a management capacity need not be re-communicated with them in a governance role, Common situation in owner-managed entities. However, it has to be ensured that communication with individuals with management responsibilities informs all of those in a governance role.

New standard is much more specific about matters that should be communicated. It is the;

- Auditor's responsibilities in relation to the audit
- Planned scope and timing of the audit
- Significant findings from the audit
- Objectives recognize importance of these matters
- Intended to increase consistency of communication practices
- Will enhance quality and effectiveness of auditor's communication with the client
- Helps the client better understand the audit and what to expect from it
- Opportunity for the client to identify any specific areas where they may ask auditor to perform additional work

- Assists auditor in better understanding the entity and its environment through dialogue with the client, consistent with the two-way communication principle
- Care needed not to compromise effectiveness of audit

Audit Report

The draft audit report can be discussed with the top executives/ HoDs. If any observation is materially wrongly mentioned and proper evidence, otherwise, is provided the same can be revisited. If necessary, some of the observations can be reworded. It is not necessary that the auditor need to yield to all the disputes of the auditee.

The final audit report can be distributed to all the concerned as per the original agreement. If the report is provided as soft copy, care should be taken that it does not land in the wrong hands. Also, a signed hard copy needs to be provided for confirmation. The major observations and recommendations can be presented to the top management.

Audit Follow-up

The control aspects of auditing are not complete until corrective action is taken or the risk formally assumed by the management. Effective statements of corrective action include;

- The specific steps to be taken
- The completion date and
- The person responsible for completion

Chapter Summary

There are 'n' number of types of audits. One among them is GRC Audit.

GRC audit on the other hand is to verify whether risk and compliance management related policies, procedures, etc., are all in place, they are updated & adequate and they are strictly followed by all the employees of the organizations.

There are five major phases of a typical audit life-cycle viz.;

- Audit Planning
- Audit Execution
- Documentation
- Communication
- Audit Follow-up

The GRC Audit is almost same as Sox-Audit in the sense that the goal of both the audits are same viz. – the policies, procedures and standards do exist within the organization. Those are adequate and UpToDate. Most importantly they are being religiously followed by every employee.

The stages to be followed in an audit depends on the knowledge of the auditor, type of audit, duration and scope of audit. However, audit and audit communication are two important stages which no auditor can skip.

*****

GRC – Business Benefits

When it comes to governance, risk and compliance (GRC), many an organization is at crossroads. On one hand, the importance of implementing effective GRC processes, is understood alongwith systems to deal with a growing range of risks and regulations. But on the other hand, they are under tremendous pressure to cut costs. However, the business benefits of a GRC program are;

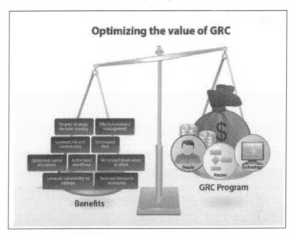

Figure 43 – GRC – Business Benefits

1.   Improved Risk Awareness – Application of the Enterprise Risk Management Framework, in conjunction with related risk management activities, augments a cultural shift to a risk-smart workforce and environment in the organization, which ensures that the organization has the capacity and tools to be innovative while recognizing and respecting the need to be prudent in protecting its interest. According to a survey on ERM, 76% of the enterprises quoted "improved awareness of risk and collaboration" as one of the major benefits. Increased risk

awareness by staff throughout the enterprise is integral to managing risk successfully.

2.   Improved Organizational Efficiency – The implementation of an ERM framework brings with its improved efficiency across the entire value chain – providing top-down coordination necessary to make various functions of an organization work efficiently. An integrated team not only better addresses the individual risks facing the company but also the interdependencies between these risks.

3.   Enhanced Shareholder Value – A strategic ERM framework brings with direct impacts to the overall profitability of a firm.

4.   Improved risk awareness and collaboration
5.   Improved regulatory compliance
6.   Improved operations
7.   Improved decision-making
8.   Reduced infrastructure, operating, or resources costs
9.   Improved earnings or shareholder value
10.   Reduced earnings volatility due to hedging
11.   Improved equity value or reduced debt costs
12.   No/ little change
13.   Standardized risk management practices across all functions and disciplines
14.   Enabled consistent, complete, and proactive coverage of risk planning, identification, analysis, treatment and reporting
15.   Moved from manual random sampling of controls to 100% testing coverage

16.   Transformation of the compliance programs to serve their business strategy while reducing their external audit hours by around 60% at the same time. "Costs can vary". "Despite the fact that Risk management software could cost an amount, depending on the size of the company and the complexity of the operation, it is not expensive. The payoff is enormous. Saving on internal costs, enhancing the credibility and streamlining risk management across the entire organization. It ultimately pays for itself.

17.   Risk Exposures Clearly Mapped – ERM enables an organization to identify measure, monitor and control its inherent risk exposures of the business at all levels. Elements like Risk Assessment, Event Management and Key Risk Indicator play an important role; enabling the organization to evaluate the risk controls, based on the identified inherent risk and to measure the residual risk which remains after the implementation of controls.

18.   Roles and responsibilities re-defined – Clearly defined roles and responsibilities within the firm's risk profile not only streamlines the risk management process, but also allows risk managers to incorporate accountability into the work culture of the organization.

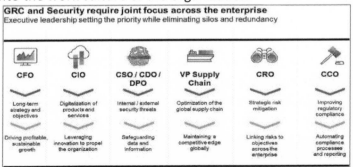

Figure 44 – GRC - Roles and responsibilities

19.   Enhance Corporate Social Responsibility (CSR) Factor – The most important outcomes of effective risk management are that it helps in "protecting and enhancing the reputation of the organization". In addition, ERM also helps in ensuring regulatory compliance and effective capital and resources allocation. Loss avoidance, increasing shareholder value and reduced earnings volatility also can be considered as some more benefits.

20.   Enhanced Profitability and Capital Allocation – Regulatory requirements such as Basel obligate banks and financial services organizations to set aside sufficient capital to act as a buffer against operational risk events. But this kind of capital allocation is not limited to banks and financial services institutions. Most organizations across industries strive to optimize capital allocation across business units in a way that is beneficial to stakeholders.

21.   Improved Resiliency – Too often, business groups performing various GRC activities tend to operate in silos with little or no collaboration or sharing of information. Any data related to risks, controls or audit data is usually managed and stored in multiple spreadsheets or in different systems. This approach not only creates silos and inefficiency, but also makes it difficult to locate data easily. The challenge is compounded if employees responsible for certain data (e.g., internal audit) leave the organization or move to a different role. If the organization then needs to access data on priority, they might have to rely on someone's memory of where that data was stored.

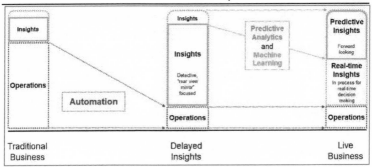

Figure 45 – Vision of GRC

With an integrated GRC system, data management becomes much more organized, efficient and convenient. All risk or compliance related data can be stored in a single, centralized, enterprise-level frame-work, making it easy and quick to find something. Organizations can consequently become more resilient to staffing changes and attrition.

Accuracy of risk and control information that enables stakeholders to make fast, risk-informed business decisions. Effective compliance programs to address constant changes in regulations, technology and the business. Consistency in GRC measures and comprehensive insights into the internal operating environment.

One other survey lists the benefits of GRC under two different headings viz. Qualitative and quantitative;

Some of the qualitative benefits;
1. Lower incidence of loss events
2. Risk threshold helps identify opportunities Risk threshold helps identify opportunities

3. Tightly manage customer credit
4. Larger number of risk factors & active monitoring
5. Reduced cost of risk management activities
6. Quantify market risks

Some of the Quantitative benefits;

1. Increase management consensus on risks
2. React faster and earlier to loss events
3. Increased company credit rating
4. Become a risk-management first mover
5. Build overall shareholder value
6. Build predictability of company performance

ERM – creating sustainable value

A majority of the respondents in the survey had companies relaying that their ERM functions produces clearly identifiable outcomes and benefits. They bring about organizational sustainability and competitive advantages;

An enhanced sense of corporate goals and objectives, talent management, significant reductions of exposure and losses. Identifying principal benefits of ERM as;

- Demonstrating compliance,
- Enhanced behavior
- Improves organizational performance and efficiency
- Helps in reducing cost of risk
- Secures growth opportunity under optimized condition.

Executives of most companies and other entities have developed processes to identify and manage risk across the enterprise and many others have begun development or are considering doing so.

A unified GRC's approach brings a high ROI for the ERM program;

- Protects and enhances the reputation of the organization
- Ensures regulatory compliance
- Ensures efficient capital and resources allocation
- Reduces earnings volatility
- Maximizes profitability of business units
- Safety of employees and customers

Over the last decade or so, many organizations have had to invest in GRC to comply with various regulations. But they have not yet realized all the benefits that GRC has to offer. They are yet to be able to look at GRC not merely as a way to avoid non-compliance penalties, but as a valuable tool to drive revenue and increase their competitive advantages.

Those are questions that each organization might find useful to ask as they develop their risk and compliance plans for the new year. No doubt, investing in GRC is not in-expensive. But the rewards gained from effective GRC processes and systems far outweigh the investments made. The key is to make GRC an integral part of organizational culture, where it percolates down into everyday business processes and decision-making at every level.

Technology also plays a significant role by simplifying GRC processes, optimizing resources, streamlining and automating workflows and enabling real-time monitoring and reporting. When technology is coupled with people and processes under the common umbrella of GRC, organizations are well-positioned to distinguish between risks and opportunities successfully — as well as to optimize costs, improve financial and operational stability and gain the trust of regulators, stakeholders, investors and customers.

Chapter Summary

The business benefits of a GRC program are;

1. Improved Risk Awareness
2. Improved Organizational Efficiency
3. Enhanced Shareholder Value
4. Improved risk awareness and collaboration
5. Improved regulatory compliance
6. Improved operations
7. Improved decision-making
8. Reduced infrastructure, operating, or resources costs
9. Improved earnings or shareholder value
10. Reduced earnings volatility due to hedging
11. Improved equity value or reduced debt costs
12. No/ little change
13. Transformation of the compliance programs to serve their business strategy
14. Risk Exposures Clearly Mapped
15. Roles and responsibilities re-defined
16. Enhance Corporate Social Responsibility (CSR) Factor

There are tangible advantages to creating this aggregated view of GRC:

 Improved alignment of objectives with mission, vision and values of the organization, resulting in better decision-making agility and confidence.

 Leverage cognitive capabilities to improve quality of information, user interaction and reduce manual tasks.

 Reduced costs in maintaining duplicated controls, tests, issues, actions and reporting across multiple disciplines.

 Reduced IT costs by consolidating on a single GRC solution.

Figure 46 – GRC Tangible benefits

*****

Appendix 1 – Abbreviations

#	Abbreviation	Expansion
1.	AI	Artificial Intelligence
2.	ATM	Automated Teller Machine
3.	BBB	Bureaucratic Black Belts
4.	BFS	Banking and Financial Services
5.	BCBS	Basel Committee on Bank Supervision
6.	BSBS	Basel Committee on Banking Supervision
7.	CEO	Chief Executive Officer
8.	CIA	Corporate Internal Audit
9.	CSR	Corporate Social Responsibility
10.	e-Banking	Electronic Banking
11.	e-Governance	Electronic Governance
12.	eGRC	Enterprise Governance Risk Management and Compliance
13.	e.g.	Example
14.	ERM	Enterprise Risk Management
15.	FI	Financial Industry
16.	GRC	Governance Risk Management and Compliance
17.	IAS	International Accounting Standard
18.	ICT	Information and Communication Technology
19.	i.e.	That is
20.	IFRS	International Financial Accounting Standard
21.	IS	Information Systems/ Security
22.	ISMS	Information Security Management System
23.	IT	Information Technology

24.	LCR	Liquidity coverage Ratio
25.	M&A	Mergers & Acquisitions
26.	MMP	Mission Mode Programs
27.	MSCI	Morgan Stanley Capital International
28.	NSFR	Net Stable Funding Ratio
29.	RWA	Risk Weighted Assets

*****

Appendix 2 – List of Figures

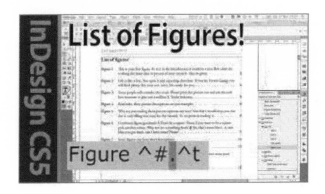

*****

About the Author
http://ramamurthy.jaagruti.co.in/

Dr. Ramamurthy (Ram) is a versatile personality having experience and expertise in various areas of Banking, related IT solutions, Information Security, IT Audit, Vedas, Samskrutam and so on.

His thirst for continuous learning does not subside even at the age of late fifties. He did his research on a very rare topic "Information Technology and Samskrutam" and obtained his Ph.D. degree. He is into a project of developing a Samskruta language-based compiler.

It is his passion to spread his knowledge and experience through conducting classes, training programs and writing books.

His already published books;

#	Title	Remarks	Pages
Indology Related			
1.	*Śrī Lalitā Sahasranāmam*	English translation of *Śrī Bhāskararāya's Bhāṣyam*	750
2.	Power of *Śrī Vidyā*	The secrets demystified – with lucid English rendering and commentaries	80
3.	*Samatā*	An exposition of Similarities in *Lalitā Sahasranāma* with *Soundaryalaharī*, *Saptaśatī*, *Viṣṇu Sahasranāma* and *Śrīmad Bhagavad Gīta*	172
4.	*Advaita* in *Shākta*	Advaita Philosophy discussed in Shaakta related Books	80
5.	*Śrī Lalitā Triśatī*	300 divine names of the celestial Mother – **English** translation of *Śrī Ādhi Śaṅkara's Bhāṣyam*	193
6.	Secrets of *Mahāśakti*	Chandi demystified	78
7.	*Daśa Mahā Vidyā*	Ten cosmic forms of the Divine mother	60

#	Title	Remarks	Pages
8.	ஸ்ரீவித்யா பேதங்கள்	ஸ்ரீவீத்யா உபாசனையின் படிகள் - கோவை ஸுதச் சண்டி மலர்	51
9.	ஸ்ரீ தேவீ ஸ்துதிகள்	பல முக்கிய அம்பாள் ஸ்தோத்ரங்கள்	133
10.	Śrī Devī Stutis – श्री देवी स्तुति:	Various important stotras of Sri Devi	
11.	ஷண்மத மந்த்ரங்கள் - षण्मत मन्त्रा:	பொள்ளாச்சி ஸ்ரீ ஸஹஸ்ரசண்டி மஹாயாக நினைவு மலர்	145
12.	Śaṇmata Mantras - - षण्मत मन्त्रा:	Important Mantras relating to Gods of six religions	87
13.	தேவதா மந்த்ரங்கள்	அக்கரைப்பட்டி ஸஹஸ்ரசண்டி மஹாயாக நினைவு மலர்	32
14.	ஆதி ஸாங்கரரும் ஷண்மதமும்	ஷண்மதங்களைப் பற்றிய ஒரு அறிமுகம்	32
15.	ஸ்ரீ ஷண்மத தேவதா அர்ச்சனை	ஸ்ரீ மஹா கும்பாபிஷேக மலர்	64
16.	Vaidhīka Wedding	Typical Wedding process in English	56
17.	வைதீகத் திருமணம்	Typical Wedding process in Tamil	57
18.	ஸ்ரீ லலிதா திரிஸதி	300 divine names of the celestial Mother – Tamil translation of Śrī Ādi Śaṅkara's Bhāśyam	234
19.	ஸ்ரீகுரு பாத பூஜா விதானம்	சித்தகிரி ஸஹஸ்ரசண்டி மலர்	44
20.	ஸ்ரீவித்யா ஸடாம்னாய மந்த்ரங்கள்	சித்தகிரி ஸஹஸ்ரசண்டி மலர்	60
21.	Ekatā	Oneness among Shiva, Vishnu and Shakti	277
22.	Vedas – An Analytical Perspective	A description of Veda, Vedanta, Vedanga, Jyotisha, Shastra, etc.	240
23.	Śrīvidya Variances	Variances in Srividya Upasana	50
24.	வேதங்கள் – ஒரு பகுப்பாய்வு	A description of Veda, Vedanta, Vedanga, Jyotisha, Shastra, etc.	280
25.	பரமாச்சார்யாள் நோக்கில் ஸ்ரீலலிதாம்பிகா	The explanation given by Paramacharya on some of the names in Lalita Sahasranama	175
26.	Ṣaṇṇavati (षण्णवति Tarpaṇa	Repaying Debts to Ancestors	42

#	Title	Remarks	Pages
27.	ஷண்ணவதி (षण्णवति தர்ப்பணம்	முன்னோர் கடன் தீர்த்தல்	48
28.	*Śrī Mahā Pratyangirā Devī*	Holy Divine mother in ferocious form	41
29.	ஸ்ரீ மஹா ப்ரத்யங்கிரா தேவீ	தெய்வீக அன்னையின் பயங்கர வடிவம்	51
30.	*Śrī Chakra Navāvarṇam*	Marvels of *Śrī Chakra*	115
31.	ஸ்ரீ சக்ர நவாவர்ணம்	ஸ்ரீ சக்ரத்தின் அதிசயங்கள்	130
32.	அம்பிகையின் (திரு) அவதாரங்கள்	ஸ்ரீ தேவியின் பல்வேறு அவதாரங்கள்	142
33.	ஸ்ரீ பிரணவானந்தர் - ஒரு சரிதம்	ஒரு அரிய ஸ்வாமிகளின் திவ்ய சரிதம்	90
Applied Samskrutam Based			
34.	*Paribhāṣā Stora-s*	An exploration of *Lalitā Sahasranāmam*	96
35.	*Śrī Cakra*, An Esoteric Approach	Mathematical Construction to draw *Śrī Cakra*	64
36.	Number System in Samskrutam	An overview of Mathematics based on Samskrutam	123
37.	*Vedic* Mathematics	30 formulae elucidated	146
38.	Vedic IT	Information Technology and Samskrutam	162
IT Based			
39.	Orthogonal Array	A Statistical Tool for Software Testing	180
Banking Based			
40.	Retail Banking	A guide book for Novice	213
41.	Corporate Banking	A guide book for Novice	232
42.	Dictionary of Financial Terms	A Guide Book for all – Demystifying Myriad Global Financial Terms	215
43.	GRC in BFS Industry	(Governance, Risk Management and Compliance by Banking & Finance Industry)	170

More books in pipeline.

Let him be wished to have a long and healthy life to share his knowledge and experiences with others.

*****

Made in United States
Orlando, FL
09 May 2023

32940359R00105